The Seeress of the *Poetic Edda* speaks of the Cosmic Tree:

I remember yet   the giants of yore
Who gave me bread   in the days gone by;
Nine worlds I knew,   the nine in the tree
With mighty roots   beneath the mold…

An ash I know,   Yggdrasil its name,
With water white   is the great tree wet;
Thence come the dews   that fall in the dales,
Green by Urth's well   does it ever grow.

The Poetic Edda, c. 1270,
translated by Henry Adams Bellows,
1936

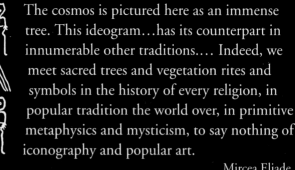

The cosmos is pictured here as an immense
tree. This ideogram…has its counterpart in
innumerable other traditions…. Indeed, we
meet sacred trees and vegetation rites and
symbols in the history of every religion, in
popular tradition the world over, in primitive
metaphysics and mysticism, to say nothing of
iconography and popular art.

Mircea Eliade,
Patterns in Comparative Religion, 1958

The tree Yggdrasill, situated at the Center, symbolizes, and at the same time constitutes, the universe. Its top touches the sky and its branches spread over the world. Of its three roots, one plunges into the land of the dead (Hel), the second into the realm of the giants, and the third into the world of men....On some not distant day, Yggdrasill will fall, and that will be the end of the world.

Obviously, we have here the well-known image of the Universal Tree, situated at the "center of the world" and connecting the three planes: Heaven, Earth, and Hades.... It could be said that Yggdrasill incarnates the exemplary and universal destiny of existence itself: every mode of existence—the world, the gods, life, men—is perishable and yet capable of rising again at the beginning of a new cosmic cycle.

Mircea Eliade,
A History of Religious Ideas,
vol. 2, 1982

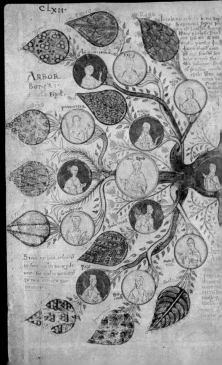

The most widespread mythical images of the "Center of the World" (traceable even in prehistory) are the Cosmic Mountain and the World Tree.... Cosmologically, the World Tree rises from the center of the earth, from the point of the earth's "navel."

Mircea Eliade,
A History of Religious Ideas,
vol. 3, 1985

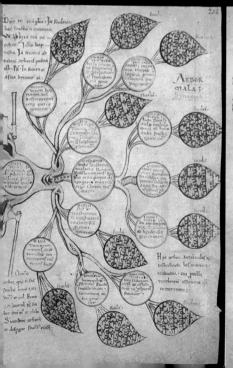

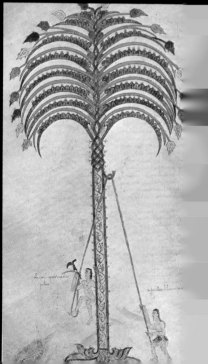

situated at the "center of the world."… In the middle of the garden stood the Tree of Life and the Tree of Knowledge of Good and Evil (Gen. 2:9). Yahweh gave man this commandment: "You may eat indeed of all the trees in the garden. Nevertheless the tree of the knowledge of good and evil, you are not to eat" (2:16–17).

Mircea Eliade, *A History of Religious Ideas,* vol. 1, 1978

Everything not directly consecrated by a hierophany becomes sacred because of its participation in a symbol. Most of the primitive symbols…are substitutes for or ways of entering into relationship with sacred objects.

Mircea Eliade,
Patterns in Comparative Religion,
1958

CONTENTS

SIGNS, SYMBOLS, AND CIPHERS

Georges Jean

DISCOVERIES®

HARRY N. ABRAMS, INC., PUBLISHERS

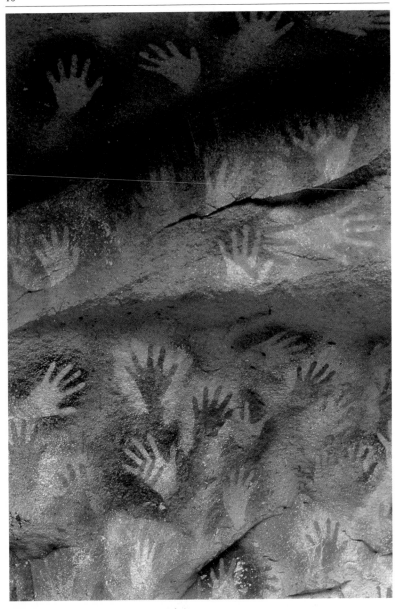

The invention of writing was a long, slow, complex process. Yet writing was neither the first nor the only means our earliest ancestors found to record ideas. Long before the appearance of this form of expression, figurative and nonfigurative images were used in pictorial systems of communication. This mode of transmitting information through signs has, since time immemorial, remained a privileged mode of discourse.

CHAPTER 1

SIGNS AS PRECURSORS OF WRITING

Left: handprints in an Argentinian cave, c. 9000–7000 BC. Similar negative handprints have been found in Paleolithic caves in Spain and France. Right: in the early 16th-century Aztec Codex Boturini, the image names as well as narrates. Chiefs are designated by signs above their heads, speak through empty scrolls that emerge from their mouths, and move in the direction indicated by footprints.

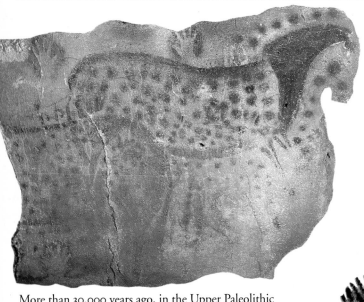

More than 30,000 years ago, in the Upper Paleolithic period, in the heart of the European regions now called France and Spain, people began to make "useless" objects: ornaments, jewelry, and especially pieces of decorated stone and bone. These tokens were marked with sequences of incisions, rhythmic lines, and dots, arranged in a certain order and with regular spacing. Such marks also began to appear on the walls of caves and shelters at about the same time. Perhaps they were simply exercises, the hand of an artisan or artist practicing dexterity. Yet we call these marks signs and are confident that they once conveyed specific meanings, though the first systems of writing were not invented until between 10,000 and 5,000 BC. We can no longer decipher their long-hidden messages; nor can we guess the reality to which they once referred. A sign, in this sense, is a line, dot, bar, rectangle, or other geometric or repeated shape thought to have a symbolic value.

Between 35,000 and 8,000 BC Paleolithic craftsmen made great drawings, paintings, relief sculptures, and engravings on the walls of caves—Lascaux in France, Altamira in Spain, and many other sites in Europe,

"To charge with meaning an abstract [visual] sign, detached from any concrete reality, is a process as powerful as that which led to the invention of writing."
Jean Abélanet,
Signes sans paroles
(*Wordless Signs*), 1986.

Africa, and Asia. Is this art? What is its purpose and meaning? Some have speculated that the images—which depict animals, human figures, handprints, objects that may be tools or weapons, and abstract marks and patterns—are artworks made by hunters. Are these images, extraordinarily alive and vividly stylized, also a language? And if so, what is it telling us?

Rock paintings as a kind of symbolic writing

The paintings and engraved figures in these Paleolithic sites form coherent groupings of visual signs. Though they are quite mysterious to us, these clusters, like a spoken or written language, express meaning in the context of the sum total of their numerous elements. Some prehistorians posit a coherent system of signs underlying these figurative and nonfigurative forms, which may express abstract ideas such as religious or mythic concepts.

Scholars often associate the pictures of animals, human hands, and other creatures with rituals related to fertility, hunting, or social ceremonies. Many specialists have

Prehistorians have noted that the abstract signs in prehistoric cave art are generally arranged in one of two ways: they are either linked to representations of animals or clustered in independent units. A painting of a horse from the cave of Pech-Merle, France, and a bison from that of Altamira, Spain, are stippled with dots, dotted lines, and parallel stripes whose meaning has not been identified. As these marks indicate, however, we may be certain that the animals are not mere decorations, but drawing-messages, or visual signs.

suggested that the more enigmatic, abstract marks in the caves—which are among the oldest drawings of all—also describe some basic themes or ideas, though all such attempts to assign meaning are extremely speculative. One idea, proposed in the 1950s, is that they represent a fundamental dialectic between the fecund feminine element and the fecundating masculine element. According to this theory, the marks are divided schematically into two groups: lines, rows of dots, and batons, which may be described as masculine, suggesting phallic forms; and ovals, triangles, and closed circles, or feminine signs, suggesting the vulva. Other theories are less categorical, and propose that the marks indicate clan or social-group identifications, or are related to religious rites carried out within caves that were not used as regular dwellings.

Signs combined to make a graphic code are writing

In general, it is thought that cave art ceased to be made gradually—some think abruptly—between 9,000 and 8,000 years ago. The cold climate that compelled humans to live in rock shelters and caves gave way in Europe to a mild and humid climate conducive to plant gathering and stock farming.

From this date on we find only a few rare bones painted or engraved with motifs, as well as painted loose rocks. A great quantity of these were found in a cave in the Pyrenees, Mas d'Azil, in 1889. These stones are flat, usually oval in shape, decorated in red or brown ocher on one or both sides, with a series of lines and dots. The number of these dots or lines, most often twenty-one or twenty-nine, has led some researchers to believe that these "signs" may note the phases of

A bove: are the geometric signs engraved on this Paleolithic perforated antler baton purely decorative, or do they perhaps identify the baton's owner, or indicate its symbolic power? No one knows. Below: in the French cave of Mas d'Azil is this enigmatic Paleolithic figure of a man pierced with wavy lines.

the moon. In the same site were found stones decorated with more complicated designs, such as axial lines intersected by one or more other lines, and broken lines that suggest letterforms.

Some historians of writing have thought that the signs depicted on these stones are an embryonic kind of writing. They may document the possession of property, or be related to counting and the recording of quantities; they may even be the manifestation of the mythic, religious, or social dialogue between the masculine and feminine principles.

But though we can imagine possibilities, we cannot assign specific meanings to any one or another of these marks, or the relations among them—that is, a graphic code, or system linking them. We thus find ourselves faced with "wordless signs," to use a term coined by the prehistorian Jean Abélanet.

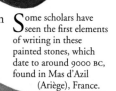

Some scholars have seen the first elements of writing in these painted stones, which date to around 9000 BC, found in Mas d'Azil (Ariège), France.

In the Bronze Age, stylized figures with many variations suggest wordless signs

By the late Neolithic period, true writing systems had developed in the Near East. But highly developed wordless sign systems had also appeared in Europe. A site at Mont Bégo, in the inhospitable mountains between France and Italy, near present-day Ventimiglia, has long been known for its Bronze Age rock drawings. These were first mentioned in a 1650 chronicle, but only beginning in the 19th century were the tens of thousands of engravings counted and catalogued. There is some indication that they were drawn over a very long period, between the Neolithic and the Bronze and Iron Ages.

The plethora of drawings and incisions

Left: an incised rock from the Bronze Age Mont Bégo site in the French-Italian Alps bears the compartment or grid motif often associated with a feminine figure and with drawings of weapons. Below: this stone from the same area displays a human figure, objects that may be spearheads or knives, and another grid motif; the scene has been interpreted—perhaps fancifully—as a cadastre protected by a warrior.

found in this area "speak" without, apparently, being a set of characters or glyphs representing words, and without sentence forms or grammar (in the linguistic sense). Figurative shapes are extremely stylized, highly varied, and almost always made with linear strokes; the images include animals, weapons, women and men performing actions with plows, horns, and tools, and what may be shelters or enclosures. Abstract geometric figures comprise circles, ovals, rectangles, empty squares, and squares enclosing series of dots or subdivided into many compartments; their significance has confounded the specialists. Jean Abélanet, in *Signes sans paroles* (*Wordless Signs*), has described these various signs in detail. He argues that as a whole they are records of rites performed by the populations that frequented these mountains in the Bronze Age. "Only religious motives," he writes, "could provoke such a profusion at such an altitude and in such a secluded spot." We cannot know this, but we may speculate that perhaps they are the vestiges of some religion tied to the mountain, the

god of the storm, or the superabundant waters in these high, isolated valleys. Other scholars have argued that the earliest written and drawn records had an economic function.

The drawings are scattered through several valleys: Val Fontalba, Valmasca, and Vallauretta, among others. Some in the Val Fontalba, composed of dotted areas linked by wavy lines, appear to record a cadastral survey, with cultivated parcels of land and access roads represented; if so, these are very ancient ancestors of cartographic representations.

More than 100,000 figures

The wall drawings and paintings in these high alpine valleys may not be true signs, as we understand the term—that is, pictorial forms that carry a symbolic reference to a thing or idea. Neither their creators nor those who "read" them are here to tell us how they were really used or what they meant. However, we may note a few salient facts about such Paleolithic and Neolithic

Above: this Bronze Age figure from Mont Bégo is an enigma. Is it human? A spirit figure? Below: images in a cave painting in Argentina.

Signs in prehistoric wall art

This series of abstract signs—some painted in red ocher, others incised into the stone surface—decorates a wall of a Paleolithic cave at El Castillo, near Santander, Spain, discovered in 1903. It comprises rows of dots and compartmented quadrilaterals of various sizes. Such geometric forms and repeated patterns are found in several French and Spanish caves, and bear very early dates. Various interpretations for them have been proposed: that they represent hunters' traps, or are cadastral records, or perhaps clan signs, similar to flags or blazons. Such meanings are purely speculative and much contested by prehistorians, but we may say, at least, that they indicate a culture familiar with symbolic imagery.

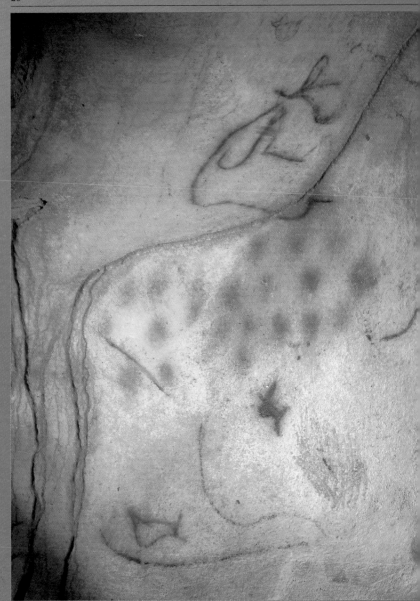

Dots and batons

Two examples of abstract signs in different Paleolithic sites. Far left: a cluster of red-ocher dots, dating to 15,000–12,000 BC, in the cave at Pech-Merle, France, discovered in 1922; right: a barbed baton in black paint and a curved, enclosed shape in red ocher, from El Castillo, Santander, Spain, 14,000–10,000 BC.

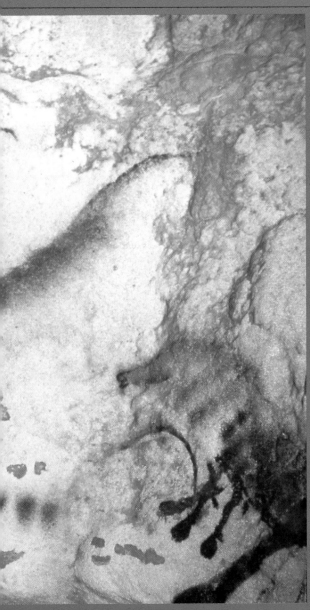

Drawings in the Lascaux cave in France combine animal images and abstract signs. A stag bears a full rack of antlers; below its head is a rectangle near a row of dots. Were these figures drawn together, or are they unrelated? Do they form a composite image with a single meaning?

"The prehistoric signs inscribed on the walls of caves, or on decorated artifacts, probably correspond to words, actions and situations which were expressed by articulate sounds in the archaic languages spoken by the Paleolithic tribes. Although to us the signs are unfathomably mysterious, they must have seemed quite the contrary to [them]. When the light from their lamps fell on a 'line of dots,' a 'quadrilateral' or a 'branched shape,' situated in a precise relationship with the figures of animals, at the beginning or end of the sequence, at the intersection of chambers or galleries, or accompanying decorated ensembles, the signs would have been translated using the spoken language.
    ...Some Paleolithic caves, notably in Spain, ...contain nothing but signs—no figures of animals at all."
Mario Ruspoli,
The Cave of Lascaux:
The Final Photographs,
translated by
Sebastian Wormell, 1987

This rock engraving at Tanum, in Sweden, dating to 1400 BC, depicts an immense masculine figure, more than 7¼ feet (2.25 meters) tall, with an erect phallus and a spear. Around him are figurative signs, including human feet and animals, and nonfigurative or geometric signs. Many interpretations of this Bronze Age image have been suggested, from a hunter's dream to a fertility totem. The size of the figure in relation to the objects surrounding him and his visible virility make one point clearly: in the ancient world men often represented themselves as masters of nature.

glyphs, especially the figures at Mont Bégo: in many sites—sometimes widely scattered—we find similar forms on numerous different documents. The repetitive nature of these figures suggests that they were conventionally recognized by their users as bearing common meanings. And while these figurative and nonfigurative, anthropomorphic and geometric figures exist in great numbers, their variations are relatively limited. Nonetheless, we cannot crack their code and are incapable of re-creating it, so that the message of these drawings remains enigmatic.

This 16th-century Native American *kiva* wall painting from New Mexico represents a warrior and is associated with rainfall, seed-sowing, and fertility. Some thirty centuries separate this image from the one on the facing page, and a comparison of the two yields some striking information. Both are large, stiffly posed, stylized, hieratic figures. The Native American painting is polychrome and depicts a man head-on, with facial features. He holds weapons and a sack, and his head is surmounted by a totem composed of crossed lines. We are far from the severity and austerity of Paleolithic art here, nor do prehistoric images usually have faces or carry containers. Thus, despite the temptation to see superficial similarities between the two images, we discover how distant these cultures really are.

Almost a writing system

We may legitimately speak of a sign system as a *writing* system when the message is delivered in a linear fashion. An interesting example of such a picture-word writing system is that developed by the Aztec. In Aztec documents such as the Codex Boturini, which dates to the time of the Spanish conquest of Mexico in the 16th century, sequences of small drawings—icons or hieroglyphs—are read literally, as ideographic pictures. Only the rudiments of a phonetic system exist. The direction of the reading, often from left to right and from bottom to top, is indicated by

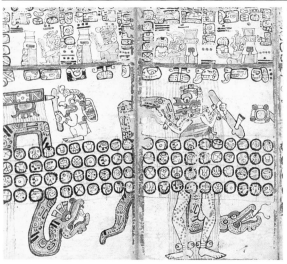

L eft: pages from the early 16th-century Maya Madrid Codex bear the sort of signs and sign series that might constitute a form of writing with words. Archaeologists have so far been able to read only numbers and the names of gods.

lines of tiny footprints. In other documents, such as the Codex Hamburgensis, which includes calendars, the direction of the reading follows a spiral.

Such drawing-messages underscore a fundamental aspect of any system of communication. It is necessary that the person receiving the message know the code or the graphic conventions used by its sender. A work of art offers only itself to the viewer and is open to any interpretation. This is not the case for drawing-messages, whose interpretations are fixed, and depend on a knowledge of the code.

Some Native North American traditions also use pictographic systems of communication. From New Mexico to the Great Lakes, a type of drawing known as picture writing has long been used to convey messages or narrate stories in a unique manner, at once graphic and linear. Among the Cheyenne and the Ojibwa picture writing was used for legal documents such as contracts of sale or trade, as well as personal letters; these figurative, or illustrative, narratives were honored as fully as documents written in language.

The native peoples of Alaska and northwestern Canada also use graphic systems of communication composed of linear suites of

pictograms. These read either from right to left or from left to right, or sometimes alternating direction from line to line in a zigzag pattern; this is known as boustrophedon and is also found in ancient Egyptian and Greek writing. These systems are related to the carved totems made by Northwest Coast Indians, as well as a few ethnic groups in central Africa, depicting the proper names of warriors and chiefs in the form of a sequence of animal figures, each of which represents a part of the name.

Mute signs, playing at times with dramatic tonalities, amplify the meaning of the message by striking the imagination

For many centuries, in most cultures of the world, writing was a skill practiced only by professional scribes and clerks, while the general population was usually illiterate. It has often been noted that the elaborate, detailed sculptures, friezes, frescoes, and stained-glass windows in the early Christian and medieval churches of Europe functioned like

Above: this fragment of a 17th-century Sioux bison-skin garment from the Dakota Territory traces the biography of a leader in the narrative form known as pictographic writing. We see him here on (literally, above) a brown horse, wielding a bow and shield.

Opposite: the figures on the totem poles of Northwest Coast Indians are much more than the symbolic representations of divinities; they are protective power figures. This Sitka carving depicts a chief whose power is emphasized by his erect phallus.

visual books, displaying scriptural narratives and sacred history in a form that the unlettered faithful could study. But even after alphabetical and phonetic writing systems were established and literate cultures developed, drawing-messages were perpetuated as a communication form. Why? Without the use of words, they convey a broad range of subtle signals, feelings, and reactions; they lead us directly from the image of the thing represented to the memory of our actual experience of that thing.

Rebuses and stories in images

The Greek historian Herodotus, writing in the 5th century BC, tells the following tale. The kings of Scythia were threatened by Darius, king of Persia. They sent him a gift of a bird, a mouse, a frog, and five arrows. Darius interpreted this gift to signify that they were surrendering to him, yielding their lands and their rivers, since the mouse lives on land, the frog lives in water, and the bird is "the likest to a horse"; the five arrows, he thought, represented the weapons of war. However, one of his companions had a different interpretation, reading the message thus: unless you become a bird and fly away through the air, a mouse and hide in the earth, or a frog and jump in a lake, you will be pierced by five arrows, and will never return home (Herodotus, *The History*, 4.131–33).

Note, first of all, that this message invites controversy and debate, though ultimately it is understood clearly. What advantage did this form of communication offer the Scythians? In showing, rather than telling, such a message sets images and reactions in play. The juxtaposition of arrows and small, fragile animals produced a dramatic effect. So

vivid an image induced the Persians to picture themselves in flight immediately, without giving them the time for critical analysis. The same message, if transmitted in

Left: a 19th-century Indian pictographic document from the Comarca de San Blas region of Panama. The text gives instructions to a singer coming to the aid of the soul of a sick person. In the center we see the sick person lying down in a tent. Around him or her are representations of objects, plants, and mythological symbols, including sun bark and medicine stones. Such polysemous images are capable of great richness and complexity of meaning.

words, might have appeared as mere empty bombast.

Mute signs are often able to say a great deal more than written texts. Sometimes writing enters a visual narrative, as in the scrolls and inscriptions of medieval paintings or the boxes and balloons of modern comic books. But there is an important difference between a comic book with text and one with no trace of writing. In the former instance, the writing anchors the meaning of the message, as the French critic Roland Barthes (1915–80) has noted; in the latter, the person receiving the information—the "reader"—constructs a story from the signs proposed by the images. His or her freedom of interpretation is thus far greater. It follows that every system of communication, written or visual, poses problems of coding and interpretation. The viewer or reader must approach any given system with the key to its code in hand; even so, interpretation is always colored by the presuppositions of both the author and receiver of the message.

Opposite: this Aztec image from the 15th-century Codex Telleriano-Remensis represents a scene from the Aztec civil war. The warrior to the right has shot the warrior at left, who was moving toward him (as indicated by the direction of the foot-prints), with an arrow. Here again, the image narrates through purely visual signs, not associated with words.

The first, primitive means of expression was the gesture. When gestures became more sophisticated, they evolved into signs. Gestural signs are inherent to humanity; they complement our spoken language, specifying or accentuating what is said. Indeed, gestures can be so efficient that they no longer accompany the word, but replace it.

CHAPTER 2
SIGNS OF THE BODY

Left: Pantaloon, a clownlike character from the old Italian Renaissance theater, uses his whole body to express avidity, desire, curiosity, cupidity. Commedia dell'arte communicates character through stylized hand and body gestures, while the face is hidden by a cartoonish mask. The French genre painter Claude Gillot (1673–1722) captures this effect. Right: a face alone is enough for the Renaissance painter Ercole de' Roberti (1449–96) to express all the world's sorrow in this face of Mary Magdalen from c. 1497.

The body speaks. Without words, without writing, we use the body to express our feelings, deliberately or unconsciously, and to communicate them to our peers. The human body is an extraordinarily complex machine, capable of a many-faceted mode of expression that uses voice, gesture, tone, vocabulary, and myriad other tools. It is beyond the scope of this study to try to unravel all the elements of that discourse. We shall content ourselves with watching the body in action— a signifying reality from which the universal forms of language emerge.

The first language of the body: the birth cry

Long before they know how to use words, human babies express themselves with their bodies and with certain vocal manifestations—weeping, cooing, complaints, laughter. An infant's much-anticipated first smile is a powerful sign, a gesture, as is the agitation that expresses dissatisfaction or anger. Babies lie down most of the time and are not yet conscious of being vertical creatures; from that horizontal position they do not know how to use their bodies in a coherent manner to make themselves under-stood. Even to those who observe a baby intently, these body signs are still mere indications and are often interpreted imprecisely. Children learn the language of the body little by little, while at the same time

Above left: the Virgin Mary, one of several figures in a 1485 *Pietà* sculpture by Niccolò dell'Arca, expresses harrowing grief with her whole body, her face, and her flying robes. Left: Saint John the Evangelist meditates, tormented and immobile. These silent figures speak the language of pure physical expression.

The French socialist orator Jean Jaurès (1895–1914) was famous for his grand, persuasive speaking style. In this 1910 painting by Eloy Vincent we see Jaurès in the tribune of the French Chamber of Deputies, demanding the floor (below right); then, using only his right hand and the weighty posture of his body, he identifies and expounds his convictions (below center). The force of these gestures, combined with magnificent speechifying, was tremendous. In 1914, on the brink of World War I, the French novelist Roger Martin du Gard (1881–1958) reported that "Jaurès had but to shout, but to make one gesture of the hand, for the fanatic crowd to hurl itself after him, heads lowered, to the assault of any Bastille whatsoever." The French philosopher Emile Chartier, known as Alain (1868–1951), described the twofold rhetoric of body and voice that a great orator could command: "He kept [the audience] at bay…; if people began to crowd close he would gaze over their heads. Then he would return his regard to them from afar, hurling his opinions at them through the air, keeping them at arm's length, perceiving them as a single mass."

acquiring the verbal signs that constitute their mother tongue.

Among adults, while the body sometimes expresses itself silently, most often body language is accompanied by verbal language. In fact, it is rare that an individual does not join gesture to speech. Gestures therefore have the role of clarifying, underscoring, supplementing, or contradicting what is said. It is notable that these plays of gesture are very often universal, as are their seconding or contradicting meanings. Although these visual signs may vary culturally and historically, all men and women of all races and all civilizations express themselves and communicate with precise body gestures and signs.

Attitude, carriage, bearing, manner, comportment, demeanor, posture, stance: the vocabulary of the body

Watch the ways the body holds itself: what are its signals? Does it look hostile or friendly, loving, reserved, indifferent, tense, easygoing, relaxed? That nebulous word *attitude* refers to movements and poses that translate psychological states or character traits into physical form. Attitudes are general and usually tied to the notion of immobility, either total or relative. Gestures, on the other hand, tend to communicate specific concepts and are associated with mobility or movement. To move is to make one or more gestures, and perhaps to change attitudes as well; but one may also change attitudes while holding quite still.

Theoreticians of language have attempted to establish a lexicon of body signs

Aside from observing and analyzing modes of comportment, researchers in the 19th century—among them Charles Darwin—tried to catalogue the elementary signs that comprise them. These students of the science known as physiognomy were especially interested in the expressions of the face and each of its units: the shape of the face; the use of its many muscles, in series, in groups, or alone; the eyes, their expressions and movements, as well

Below left: *La Lettre attendue* (the long-awaited letter) is the title of this poster from the late 19th century. Exaltation, joy, tenderness…words cannot describe the facial and gestural expressions of this old couple.

as the movements of the eyelids and eyebrows; and so on. To raise the brows is a sign, as is to blink the lids, quickly or slowly. The movements of the mouth, apart from the formulation of verbal language, convey infinitely diverse and varied meanings. As for facial expressions, or panto-mime, these include universal signs, such as those making a smile or expressions of anger or attention, while others are culturally determined. Universal signs are so powerful

"The face is so complex, with the capability of hundreds of minor ten-sions and relaxations, tuggings and pullings, that it can express a change in underlying mood while hardly altering at all…"
Desmond Morris,
Manwatching, 1977

that in many cultures people substitute painted faces for natural ones for aesthetic or religious reasons, as we see in the symbolic make-up used in Chinese and Japanese theaters, and in many masking traditions.

Hands likewise constitute a vast reservoir of potential signs, either alone or in combination with other body parts. One example is the very common way direction is indicated: the hand is raised and posed, fingers are folded, and one points in the direction; all this is often accompanied by a movement of the head. The head, whose range of motion is principally left-right and up-and-down, plays an important role in this body language. Every part of the body contributes to this wordless language. In general, the easiest gestural codes to create and understand are those made with the movements of the fingers and hands. We shall explore these in depth shortly, when we examine sign languages used by the deaf and by Trappist monks.

In addition to conveying literal meanings, body language has ethical and aesthetic ramifications in all cultures. Gestures can be not

Above left: the face of this Kathakali dancer from India is painted in a set, traditional pattern. The tiara is the sign of a royal personage.

only meaningful or meaningless, and truthful or dishonest, but beautiful or ugly. Think of the highly stylized postures used in fashion photographs and the classic poses of painters' and sculptors' models.

Body language is the core vocabulary of dance, and dances of all kinds obey codes—the grammar of the body, so to speak. The rigorous formal code of classical ballet, for example, is based on aesthetic principles; the symbolic codes in the dances of Bali, Java, and India, whose precise elements may be read like words in a book, are based on both aesthetic and religious principles. Many traditional Indian dances rely heavily on a detailed vocabulary of hand and finger positions called *mudras*.

Among all the gestural languages around the world, which are countless, it is interesting to linger a little on two closed and rigorously coded systems: the gestural language of Trappist monks, who take vows of silence, and the modern sign languages of deaf people.

Cloistered monks renounced speech and communicated with gestures

The 6th-century religious Saint Benedict, founder of many monasteries, wrote in his Rule concerning monastic life that monks should avoid speech. When communication was indispensable, he suggested, they should use a substitute, "some sound or sign." The systematic use of gestures in the Benedictine order is mentioned for the first time around the year 1000, and the first list of these gestures contains 296 signs. Over time other lists evolved, and with the foundation of the Trappist order, which is fully silent,

Costume, makeup, gestures, and body poses all are part of the actor or dancer's repertoire of communicative tools. Below left: an American Indian Eagle Dancer from Iowa, painted in the 1920s; center: an actor of the traditional Kabuki theater of Japan; below: a sculpture of a Tibetan divinity performing a ritual dance with *mudras*. These stylized movements and positions of hands and fingers are rigorously traditional and constitute a defined language for many of the peoples of South and East Asia.

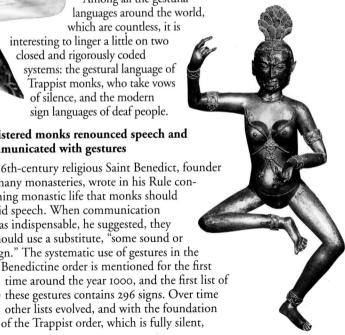

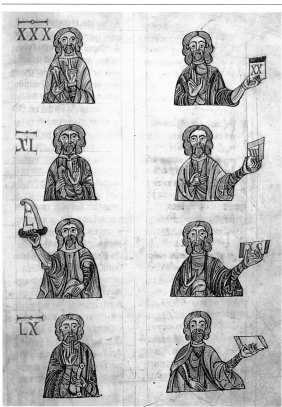

monastic sign language came to comprise about 1,300 signs. These can be classified in four categories: interrogation, command, desire, and affirmation.

Since the invention of modern linguistics, sign languages have been analyzed in very sophisticated terms: the sign is called the signifier, the carrier of meaning. The meaning is called the signified. In monastic sign language, as in most codes, we usually encounter signs (signifiers) in direct relation to their meaning (the signified). For example, making the sign of the Cross refers to—or represents—the Cross itself, and indicates a blessing or prayer. But other signs have no direct, representational relationship to their meaning; these signs are arbitrary

Left: in this 9th-century German manuscript a sage counts on his fingers while the numbers themselves hover nearby.

Saint Benedict admonished his monks to "communicate with gestures." Above: Cistercian signs for *late, master of novices,* and *food.*

or more simply conventional. Hence, to express *half* one touches the midpoint of the index finger, which is in direct relation to the signified; but to indicate *one quarter* one touches the end of the index finger, because it would be too ambiguous to indicate one quarter of the finger, since the finger joints naturally divide it into three. Highly developed sign languages make use of both representational and abstract signs.

Simple and compound signs

For the signified *bee* (Trappist monks were often beekeepers), the gesture for *wing* is combined with the one for *sweet*. For the word *honey,* the gesture for *butter* is combined with the compound gesture for *bee*. In other cases two movements are combined. For *metal,* the indicated gesture is to pass the extended index and middle fingers over the left index frequently, as if rubbing with a file. To add the sign *hard,* one presses the back of the hand with the joint of the middle finger. Trappist signs designate objects, movements, and ideas closely bound to the bucolic religious lives of the monks.

Two observations can be made: the list of these words is relatively short, and one cannot say everything using it. Moreover, there is no alphabet of any sort with which one might augment the permitted gestures. All the gesture-signs refer directly and concretely to established meanings, so that communication is restricted. Because the system seems to have developed empirically, as need arose, there are also many unclear signs that give rise to ambiguous situations.

This twofold observation helps us better to grasp the problems posed by the visual sign languages used by the deaf. There are virtually as many of these as there are spoken equivalents, and

In this 15th-century Italian fresco Saint Benedict stands immobile, fingers to his mouth and book open: signs expressing his rule of silence.

many are fully inflected, complete linguistic systems. These are generically called Sign. British Sign Language (BSL) and American Sign Language (ASL) are two that are widely used. Unlike Trappist signing, both these systems are fully capable of translating any written or spoken language into gestural form; like British and American spoken English, they are not identical. Sign uses both symbolic gestures that represent whole words or concepts and those that represent letters of the alphabet. With the latter, in a technique called finger spelling, words are spelled out for which no iconic (representational or abstract) gesture exists. Though in some respects Sign has a certain internationality, and elements of American or British Sign might be understood by, for example, a Polish user, these languages are as culturally specific as a spoken tongue. There is also a fully international language called Gestuno, developed in 1975 on the Esperanto model. It uses only icon gestures and creates new ones for new concepts. It is entirely detached

Every language of the world has its own version of Sign. Below: a diagram shows an early form of Sign language, in which words are spelled out letter by letter, with a manual alphabet. Opposite below: the Abbé de l'Epée, in the early 19th century, espoused a system of hand gestures representing whole words and ideas; the two concepts were later combined in the modern system.

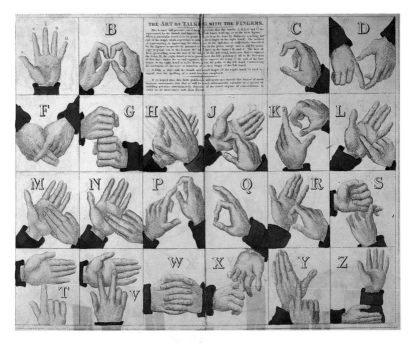

THE ART OF TALKING WITH THE FINGERS.

from the alphabet of any written language, but is more limited expressively, and may be described as a very fluid, flexible code, rather than a complete language. In Europe some advocates are developing an International Sign Language, or ISL, which has the attributes of national-language-based Sign languages. There has long been a debate between proponents of these two approaches as to their relative efficacy, completeness, and independence from spoken languages.

The story goes that a French cleric, the Abbé Charles Michel de l'Epée (1712–89), once took shelter from the rain in the house of twin deaf-mute sisters. Living together for a long time, they had empirically created a remarkable system of communication through signs. Impressed, the Abbé created a systematic version of this language, reproducing in gestures the syntax and grammar of a spoken tongue.

L'Epée deserves a lot of credit, but he did not understand that it was not necessary to reproduce the syntax and linear

An early form of finger spelling, proposed by J.-P. Bonet, 1620: the letters *H, I,* and *L.*

structure of spoken language in all its abstract complexity. In fact, what makes the modern languages of the deaf so original and innovative is that their corporeal and spatial structure differs radically from that linear structure.

The languages called Sign are each a coherent, effective, self-referential ensemble of gestures. As such they are interesting from a theoretical perspective, demonstrating that a true language, with its own syntax, grammar, lexicon, and style, may be composed solely of gestural signs. Sign languages are based on simple codes and use a relatively reduced (and hence economical) number of parameters. To express the sign *happy* in one system, for example, these parameters are as follows: configuration (position of the hand); orientation (of the hand: palm turned toward the body); spatial placement (where the sign is made: the chest); movement (circular); expression on the face (joy). On the basis of these delimited parameters, Sign creates a complete dictionary. The language is capable of expressing the full range of nuances that spoken languages command, including poetry, regionalisms, and slang.

Mixing gestural sign language with speech

The Sioux, a North American Indian nation from the Great Plains, once used both a spoken language and a gestural one. This unvoiced form of expression is apparently very ancient; indeed, it may even be the oldest North American language.

The Siouan sign language includes between 450 and 500 signs, almost all made with the hands (either still or

The Sioux invented a very complete gestural language. Left to right: *beaver, friend, stag.*

in motion), the face, and the position of the head. These include nouns, adjectives, verbs, and adverbs, forming a true language, but the Siouan sign vocabulary is limited to subjects relating to hunting and war. This gestural language does not create a true code of signs, like Sign language, but rather an ensemble analogous to that of the Trappist monks. All three of these language systems serve closed, self-referential communities. They have in common the fact that they do not rely on the alphabet. Through the visual symbolism of the gesture, the distinction between signifier and signified is blurred.

Creating signs in relief that the blind read with their fingers

In 1784 Valentin Haüy (1745–1822), a French specialist in decoding manuscripts, founded a school for blind

Left: two pages of a 1925 braille book on music; the right-hand page shows both standard musical notation and the braille equivalents. Above: Valentin Haüy, teacher of Louis Braille, who invented an alphabet for the nonsighted still in wide use today. Braille had the genius to understand that a dot system would be far clearer to the touch than letterforms, which are essentially understood visually. Dots of a uniform size are also easy and quick to prick, or emboss, into paper, and Braille perfected the use of this raised writing technique, based on ideas of Haüy. Haüy was sighted; Braille, being himself blind, was able to conceive of a system most readily suited to his needs.

children. In 1791 he invented a form of writing for the blind using embossed characters. For the nonseeing this represented considerable progress, but the system of relief characters was imperfect, prone to errors and confusions. In 1819 a 10-year-old boy, Louis Braille (1809–52), entered Haüy's institute. A precocious child, he studied sonography (related to what we call Morse code), in which

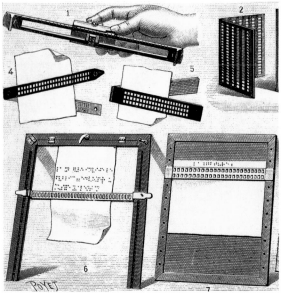

sounds or seismic vibrations are transcribed into written symbols with phonetic values and used to convey information. At the age of 20 he used this concept to invent a relief writing system based not on characters but on groups of dots in 63 combinations. These comprise an alphabet, numerals, the main mathematical signs, and musical notation. A braille reader sweeps the tips of the fingers across a page embossed with these raised dots. The system is efficient and fast: most readers develop a sensitive touch and can read about 150 words a minute, on average.

Initially, the printing of books in braille was time-consuming and costly, with pages laboriously pricked by hand. Today, texts are transcribed into braille

Braille's dot alphabet is read with the sensitive tips of the fingers. Like most western writing systems, it is written in parallel horizontal lines from left to right. Once the alphabet itself was perfected, apparatuses had to be designed to permit unsighted writers to compose texts easily. Braille signs, made of clusters of dots, must be made with precision and spaced evenly in lines, while the lines themselves must also be aligned evenly. Sloppy writing in braille is even harder to read than messy script. Left: early braille writing instruments—grids, a punch, and a movable sliding ruler, fitted on a frame. Books in braille are extremely large, made of a tough, flexible paper that can take an embossment but will not easily be punched through. Today, books recited on audiotapes are popular, but they are expensive to make and often abridged; many blind readers, like those who are sighted, much prefer the quiet privacy of reading.

mechanically, and the advent of the computer has made transcription ever more efficient.

Unlike the gestural languages examined above, braille is a direct transcription of the alphabet, and exists in all written languages that use an alphabet. As a sign system it is also unique in one fascinating respect: most other alphabets and writing systems use a combination of lines, curves, dots, and compound marks to create their letterforms, but braille uses only one basic sign: the dot. Formally, it is thus extremely simple (and simple to use), and purely abstract, with no vestige of the sort of iconic symbolism that still connects certain written figures to the pictures they may once have been: the zero linked to an empty circle, or the letter *O* to an open mouth forming that sound.

We communicate through a complex of body signs, hand and face gestures, writing, and speech

The play of human relations relies on a network of links between words and the body's more subtle forms of language. A gesture, a mimed image, a glance —these have their own syntax and grammar; we may lie or tell the truth as well with silent expressions as with words. We can appreciate the deliberate, meditative silence, peopled with a few spare, poetic gestures, that Trappist monks have chosen for their highly symbolic language. Equally, we understand the preference of nonhearing people to emerge from silence through a uniquely physical language that engages the whole body and being in the act of communication.

The invention of braille freed blind people not only to read, but also to write. Below: an early braille typewriter, known as the Mauler (after the name of its inventor). The writer turns a wheel bearing the braille alphabet signs, which he identifies with the tips of his fingers. Then, pressing down on a lever, he prints each letter with one stroke. Since the invention of this brilliant machine, electric machines have been perfected that do much the same thing. Braille is an international writing system, adaptable to any language that uses an alphabet.

In war—or any situation that calls for urgent action—we need to send and receive information rapidly. To transmit signs and signals from afar, without distorting meaning, has been a universal objective of communication systems through the ages.

CHAPTER 3
THE MAGIC OF LONG-DISTANCE SIGNS

Left: a fire signal is one of the oldest methods of sending a long-distance message, but it is unreliable and limited. Who knows if this marooned 19th-century damsel in distress will ever be rescued? Right: Fire works well at night, but for daylight signals, a flag is better, if it is high enough to be seen from far away. These 19th-century telegraphers have rigged an ingenious pulley system for signaling ships at sea.

Communication theory defines *noise* as any sound (or other event) that attaches itself parasitically to a transmission and causes a loss or distortion of information during the process of communication. Noise may be accidental or deliberate. From the moment the message leaves its source (the transmitter) until the moment it is received by the recipient (the receiver), noise may interrupt at any time: during the transmission of the message itself or during coding and decoding.

One means of compensating for the problem of noise and facilitating the good reception of messages is to send a

Sound signals, such as those trumpeted by this medieval watchman (left) announcing the return of soldiers, and visual signals, such as the torches of these soldiers in ancient Greece (below left, in an illustration of the 1920s), have always been useful in war. Greek fire signals are thought to have had different meanings, depending on the placement of the torches behind the battlements.

message more than once. For the same reason, redundancy is also often employed in the design of codes, languages, or sign systems used for sending information: certain elements may recur or be combined, in order to simplify the system and make it easier to receive. For example, braille, using the dot as its single recurring element, reduces the chances of misinterpretation or error in decoding.

The first systems of long-distance signals used rudimentary codes

In the 19th century—and probably much earlier—some Native American peoples used smoke signals. The most widespread codes, among the Sioux and the Cheyenne, for example, were very simple. One puff of rising smoke

Lovers of Westerns are well acquainted with the language of smoke signals of the North American Indians, imagined here by Frederic Remington (1861–1909). They covered and uncovered a small fire with skins, in order to send up puffs, streams, and rounds of smoke whose shape, number, and rhythm alerted friends to danger or called for help.

meant "attention"; two meant "all is well"; and three puffs, or the appearance of flames, meant "danger, call for help." The puff of smoke was made by covering and uncovering a fire, usually with cloth or skins.

Fire seems to be the most ancient medium of long-distance signaling, since smoke rises and is visible from far off in daylight, while fire beacons are visible at night. Numerous ancient sources refer to such methods. The classical Greek tragic poet Aeschylus, writing around 458 BC in the *Agamemnon,* describes a watchman on the palace roof in Argos, waiting for the signal fire that will bring news of the distant war at Troy: "I wait; to read the meaning of that beacon light, a blaze of fire to carry out of Troy the rumor and outcry of its capture.... Now let there be again redemption from distress, the flare burning from the blackness in good augury."

The Talmud, written around AD 400, alludes to a network of communication between the cities of Jerusalem and Babylon, separated by some 500 or 600 miles (nearly 1,000 kilometers) of desert. Relay fires were lit on a chain of towers and mountaintops. It is thought that the code was based on the dura- tion of the fires lit and the height of the flames; but this is speculation.

One may imagine that elementary smoke and fire signals were quite confusing. Their expressive range was limited to a few simple concepts

The ringing of bells according to a schedule has long been a way of marking the passage of time in a village. Aside from the call to religious services, bells signal dawn and sunset, announce baptisms, marriages, and deaths (through the somber rhythm of the knell); in the case of fire, cataclysm, or war, they sound the tocsin. Left: a 12th-century bell ringer from a church in France.

Below: ringing bells are not the only socially recognized sound code; in Switzerland a shepherd's alpine horn makes a deep, loud sound whose significance is intelligible only to other local shepherds, though it is heard by all the people in the neighborhood.

and dependent on a clear agreement between parties on the conventions of signals. Distant smoke might indicate nothing more than a farmer burning off fields, or a lightning strike after a storm. Yet long-distance communication relied on such systems—or others that were little better, such as postal services with teams of relay horses—for many centuries. Not until the modern era did technology provide new ways of communicating.

The Enlightenment fosters long-distance communication; the French Revolution accelerates its technical advances

The word *telegraph* comes from Greek roots meaning "long-distance writing." With the growth of scientific experiment in Europe in the 17th and 18th centuries and the invention of many new tools and mechanical devices, scientists began to dream of machines to convey information quickly over great distances. In 1684 the English physicist and philosopher Robert Hooke (1635–1703) tried to perfect a system of optical telegraphy (that is, messages transmitted visually over a long distance). In 1690 a French physicist, Guillaume Amontons (1663–1705), proposed a network of international signal devices: people with telescopes were to sit in a chain of consecutive observation posts between Paris and Rome; each, seeing signals from the preceding post, would relay them to the next; the signals themselves were in an alphabet code whose solution was possessed only in the first and last posts. The sight range of a telescope

Light signals may employ fires, electricity, or the sun. Above: soldiers send Morse code with electric lamps; left: an optical telegraph station from about 1840 uses a set of swiveling mirrors to send dots and dashes of sunlight; below: French soldiers in 1907 use an optical-telegraph telescope.

defined the distance between posts and the minimum number of posts necessary to cover the distance (about 700 miles, or 1,100 kilometers). "People might find it whimsical, though brilliant," wrote the poet and historian Bernard Le Bovier de Fontanelle (1657–1757), "this means he invented to say everything desired from a great distance, from Paris to Rome, for example, in a very short time, such as three or four hours, and without the news being known in the places in between. This proposition, as paradoxical and chimerical as it might seem, was executed in a small stretch of land…"

Other inventors in the 18th century tried various forms of mechanical telegraph, coded and uncoded, but these systems would probably long have remained mainly experimental,

Chappe's telegraph semaphores had to be installed high up, in order to be seen well. Here, French citizens wearing the tricolor ribbons and cockades of the Revolution observe a Chappe semaphore in action on a specially constructed tower.

had not the French Revolution of 1789 sparked a series of wars that entangled most of Europe. Commanders needed to communicate with their armies at the front secretly and quickly. Too often, mounted couriers were intercepted or captured and their messages lost. Military authorities in France, England, and elsewhere became interested in what had been until then a purely intellectual and commercial pursuit.

Semaphore and telegraph signs

Semaphore (from the Greek *sema,* or sign) is a technique of visual signaling over a distance, using flags (as in ship-to-ship communications), lights (as in railway signals), other mechanical devices, or even motions of the arms (this is known as wigwagging). In France in 1794, at the height of the Revolution, the Chappe brothers, Claude (1763–1805) and Ignace-Urbain-Jean (1760–1829), established a telegraphic line between Paris and Lille, using semaphore signals and telescopes. The novelty of their system lay less in the creation of the line

In the early 1800s the medieval church of Saint-Pierre de Montmartre, on the highest hill of Paris, bore a Chappe optical telegraph semaphore on its truncated tower. It was furnished with a mechanical transmitter (which moved the signal arms) and manned by an observer (visible on the balcony), who used a spyglass to receive signals from other posts.

Signal Dactiule

*Ce signal a pour objet d'a-
vertir les stationaires que l'on va
Commencer la transmission il est
indiqué par la premion horison-
tal du Regulateur et par le
developement des deux ailler a
quatre vingt dix degrex vers le
Ciel,*

The great cleverness of the Chappe system lay in its code. One could express a large number of discrete figures by manipulating the positions of the transmitter's arms in different combinations. The operator sat in a small room below the semaphore and executed signals on a miniature version of the signaling apparatus that was linked to the big one; each movement and position was transmitted mechanically to the external machine.

than in the code they perfected. The semaphore device itself was a pole bearing at its top a transverse bar, to whose ends were fastened arms that could be swiveled into various positions, each of which represented words or letters. These semaphores were placed in a series running from one city to the other. The coded system of 196 signs invented by the Chappes was remarkable for its originality and semiological inventiveness.

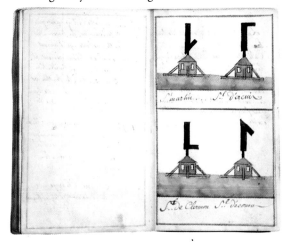

These pages are from Claude Chappe's original code book of 1794, which explained and illustrated his system. Under the National Convention (1792–95) the Chappe telegraph was first used for military purposes by the Revolutionary armies.

The Chappe brothers next developed a more sophisticated cipher system. They produced a 92-page lexicon, each page of which had 92 words, each of these identified by a number. The first signal sent by the telegrapher indicated the page in the lexicon; the second, the number on the page corresponding to the word in the dispatch. Using simple pairs of number signals in this way, one could send messages with a vocabulary of 8,464 words.

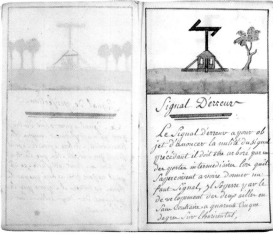

A B C
D E F
G H I
K L M
N O P
Q R S
T U V
W X Y
Z & 1
2 3 4
5 6 7
8 9 10

They then created a second 92-page lexicon, each page this time containing 92 sentences or phrases, for a total of 8,464 concepts, mostly relating to the navy and army. To use this lexicon, the telegrapher sent sets of three number signals: the first to indicate that the sentence-book, rather than the word-book, was being used; the second to indicate the page; and the third for the phrase on the page. Another lexicon listed place names and other geographical terms.

This is a striking example of how effective a coherent code of signs may be when it is designed to serve a specific need.

New telegraph systems generate new codes

The Chappe system required an infrastructure: a network of semaphores situated about 6 to 18 miles (10 to 30 kilometers) from one another, depending on the terrain. The stations had to be placed on raised sites (hills, tall buildings, bell towers), so that the signals could be seen by telescope. Like all optical telegraphs, its performance depended on weather conditions. In times of fog, rain, or storms, or in the glare of too bright a sun, it was unusable.

Telegraphy improved rapidly with the first experiments in electricity. In 1746, in England, William Watson (1715–87) had transmitted an electric current through a length of wire, and in America in the same year Benjamin Franklin (1706–90) had made similar demonstrations; soon thereafter physicists in England,

Left: the first code used for the Chappe telegraph comprised 36 signs, representing alphabet letters (in old French no distinction is made between I and J), numerals, and an ampersand. Basic messages were easy to compose.

The Chappe optical telegraph was able to transmit maximum meaning efficiently and secretly. Its method was economical: with a limited number of signs, detailed messages could be transmitted and received. Interception and deciphering of transmitted dispatches were very difficult, for only the initial transmitter and the final receiver knew the code. The lexicons served as cipher books and did not circulate. Morse code and many modern computer codes are easier to crack.

Opposite: the mechanical semaphore consisted of a tall wooden pole, or mast, topped by a crossbar on a pivot. At each end of this bar were two smaller arms, also on pivots. The joints of this contraption were maneuvered by means of a pulley system, and the entire object could be swiveled on its base in four distinct directions, to present different profiles to the observer.

France, Switzerland, and elsewhere developed primitive telegraphs that sent signals electrically, along grounded wires. At the end of the 18th century discoveries by the Italian physicists Luigi Galvani (1737–98) and Alessandro Volta (1745–1827) concerning the properties of electricity—especially their experiments in continuous current and the storage of current in reservoirs—made true electrical telegraphs possible. In the first half of the 19th century several such systems were tested, notably those of the Americans Joseph Henry (1797–1878) in 1830 and Samuel F. B. Morse (1791–1872) in 1837 and the Englishmen Charles Wheatstone (1802–75) and William Fothergill Cooke (1806–79), also in 1837. All these systems transmitted intelligible signals by means of an electrical current, but each inventor fashioned his own set of signs and codes to suit his particular mechanism. In Wheatstone's system, for example, an electrical current stimulated a magnetic needle to deviate along a dial, indicating a letter of the alphabet. The letter on the receiving dial matched that on the transmitting dial; his sign system therefore belongs to the code of writing, laboriously spelled out, letter by letter.

Morse's system is relayed according to an entirely different principle, though it too is predicated on the concept of the alphabet. Abandoning the idea of a magnetic needle wavering on a dial, he based his code on the rhythmic interruption of the current. Morse code is both original and beautifully simple: the signs are all composed of various combinations of only two elements, the dash and the dot, each group of dots and dashes representing a letter of the alphabet in a manner akin to the code of braille dots. These dots and dashes were tapped out on a simple instrument that broke the continuous flow of electric current for short and long instants, as it was being transmitted. The dot-dash-dot of the Morse transmitter is exceptionally communicable: it can be heard as long and short notes or beeps, read as marks printed on a band of paper, or seen as long and short bursts of light. It was fast and easy to send over an electrical wire—a natural vehicle for telegraphic messages; it was simple to learn; and in its blinking-light form it was (and still is) convenient for communication at night or at sea. Indeed, it was soon adapted for naval use in a somewhat more complex system of colored flags, waved at different

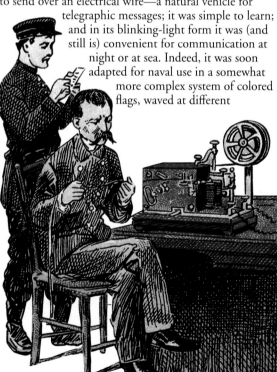

F (Az íröszeg. G (Papirszalag. H (Pap
  (Schreibstift.   (Papierstreifen.   (P.

(Alphabet.)

n ▬ •
o ▬ ▬ ▬
ö ▬ ▬ • •
p • ▬ ▬ •
q ▬ ▬ • ▬
r • ▬ •
s • • •
t ▬
u • • ▬
ü • • ▬ ▬
v • • • ▬
w • ▬ ▬
x ▬ • • ▬
y ▬ • ▬ ▬
z ▬ ▬ • •

(Lith. Anstalt v. W Schreiber in Esslingen)

T he Morse telegraph (above left, a 1910 tapper) is a simple instrument. Short or long taps interrupt the electric current and transmit dashes and dots to the receiver. Morse was commonly received on a wheeled instrument (left) that recorded dots and dashes on a strip of paper.

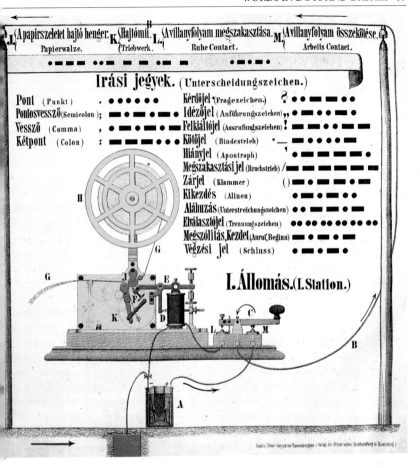

positions, which had the advantage of being international. Even today, the universal signal of distress remains a Morse code: the two simplest letters of Morse's alphabet, *S* and *O*, continuously repeated in alternation —dot-dot-dot, dash-dash-dash, dot-dot-dot, or SOS.

In 1895 the Italian engineer Guglielmo Marconi (1874–1937) invented the first system of wireless telegraphy, or radio, and inaugurated a new era of long-distance communication—one that still relies on codes, though less visibly.

Above: Morse codes for German and Hungarian, from a 19th-century schoolbook of the Austro-Hungarian Empire. The Morse alphabet varies according to the language used, for Morse, like braille, is not a language but a sign system that encodes a language for easy transmission.

Electrical signals travel through space

In the 20th century new technologies have revolutionized long-distance communications. Words and images fly into space in radio waves and circle the world at speed in the form of lines of binary computer code. Vast quantities of information are converted into an international language

By the 20th century wireless telegraphs had been developed, using the technology of electromagnetic, or radio-wave transmission. Below: a 1903 wireless station.

of surpassing simplicity: instead of using Morse's dots and dashes, we contact one another in 0s and 1s. And from the heart of the cosmos we receive strange, unreadable signals that travel to earth in the form of electrical impulses and radio waves, still awaiting the creation of a cipher book that can decode them.

In 1923 this fabulous apparatus, ancestor of the facsimile machine, sent a photographic image from Berlin to Munich. The transmitter is at left, the receiver at right.

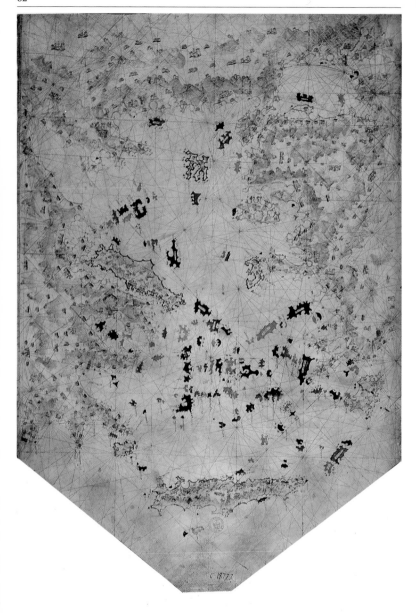

C 18727

Maps respond to our eternal need to know where we are. The graphic codes that they use have evolved over time, while developments in scientific and technical methods of measurement and graphic design have refined their capacity for abstraction. From the old landscape-style maps of the Middle Ages to contemporary computer-generated maps, the signs used in cartography have evolved in fascinating ways.

CHAPTER 4

MAPS: HOTBEDS OF SIGNS

"When one looks at a certain object only as representing another, the idea one has of it is a sign. This is usually how one looks at maps and paintings... Hence one can say, spontaneously and nonchalantly,...that a map of Italy is Italy."
Antoine Arnauld,
Logique de Port-Royal,
1872

Left: an early navigation map of the Aegean Sea, showing the Cyclades islands, Crete, and the Greek and Turkish coasts; right: a Renaissance map of the district south of Florence, *Capitani di Parte*, vol. 121.

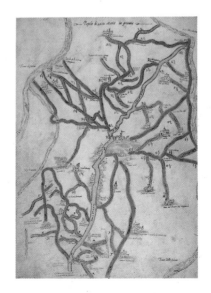

Maps are a complex agglomeration of signs, conveying concrete information about a place in abstract terms. Our approach to them is twofold and even contradictory: we both look at them as visual objects and read them as texts.

A map is a picture seen at a glance, a text read quickly

On a big sheet of paper we see a large blank area with

A map is both an instrument and an image. An instrument-map is intended for immediate practical use, while an image-map is both symbol and illustration. Early instrument-maps were rough sketches of a small, local territory, more-or-less faithfully reproducing its salient physical features. An image-map not only satisfies the basic need to locate and describe geographic details, but creates a complex, schematic portrait of it. In the medieval period the mysterious areas beyond known borders of image-maps were often peopled with fabulous monsters, dragons, and other mythological creatures. Left: detail of a 1537 portulan, or sea chart, by the Cretan cartographer Giorgio Calapoda, showing Iceland's volcanoes (including the famous Hekla), sulfur mines, and fisheries.

meandering, frilled edges. It is colored pale blue and surrounded by patches in other bright colors; these are decorated with crisscrossing straight and irregular lines and thin blue squiggles, and peppered with dots and words of different sizes, in different typefaces: we are looking at a representation of a sea with its coastal land masses (see page 128). A viewer familiar with how maps work may be able to guess the name of the sea and the scale of the image, or can learn them by reading an inscription in one corner that bears a printed name: THE MEDITERRANEAN SEA. Some people see a map as a picture first, and read it as a text second. Others first read its data and then decipher its imagery.

A map contains layers of information, some of it in words, numbers, and symbols, some in shapes, patterns,

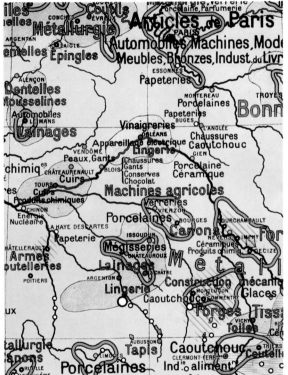

The map maker is landscape artist and scientific organizer of data, surveyor and stylist, and above all rhetorician. Within the conventions of how a map expresses information, every cartographer creates a distinct vision of the world. The figurative representation of natural signs that we see in the Iceland map (opposite) represents one extreme of realistic style (save for its inattention to the relative scale of objects); at the other end of the spectrum is the modern map that uses highly abstracted conventions. Hierarchical, orderly, and readable, it renounces the imprecision of the image-map in favor of a didactic clarity. Left: detail of a modern map of France by Jean Brunhes and Deffontaines, with color codes for manufacturing zones and labels for place names and principal industries: *Dentelles,* lace; *Machines agricoles,* farm equipment; *Tapis,* tapestry carpets, and so forth. The relative importance of each trade is indicated by size of label and by colors.

colors, and lines. Depending on what particular facts we want to glean from this piece of paper, we may begin analyzing it in one of several ways: we may observe its pictorial qualities—its beauty and expressiveness, its wealth and variety of content. Or we may turn directly to reading the various kinds of words and figures scattered across it. This latter reading is indispensable for finding one's bearings, but it may make us ignore

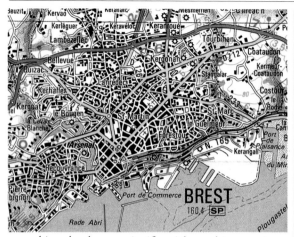

everything else the map signifies. A hasty driver, anxious to reach a distant destination on a snowy night, reads only the itinerary, the number of miles or kilometers to go, the difficulties of the route.

We read a map, but our reading is not linear, with one word following another, one sentence following another sequentially. A map's written code is spatial; words are read in relation to their position on the page and their proximity to pictorial features. And maps use a second written code: that of the key or legend, which designates a map's subject and scale, and the meaning and hierarchy of the conventional signs that represent its topographic elements—towns, roads, railways, mountains, rivers— and abstract elements, such as political borders, populations, or rates of change.

Another approach to map reading begins with the decoding or interpreting of its nonverbal signs. One can best assess how these cartographic signs work on a "mute" map, one that conveys its information without words, using signs alone to indicate places, topographic features, and other data.

Maps without word labels may tell us about topography, geography, or any number of other physical and territorial concepts; but they cannot give us the names of places. For example, we may know by a clustering of the conventional sign for *mountain* that we are looking at a

From a wealth of data about a place a cartographer chooses what to illustrate. Above left: a modern map in 1:1,000,000 scale describes the French port city of Brest in flat, schematic terms, with major arteries in bright colors (yellow for streets; red for highways), neighborhoods labeled by name, and topography represented only by faint red contour lines.

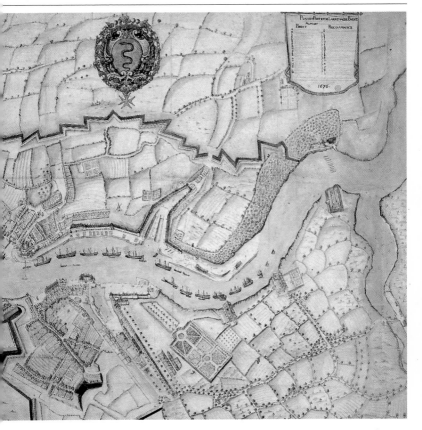

map of a mountain range. The shape of that cluster may suggest a particular, known chain of peaks, but only words can specify, or anchor, those signs to an exclusive meaning, telling us that we are looking at the Swiss Alps, or the Rocky Mountains. Similarly, a political map depends upon names to give its visual configurations meaning; after all, borders between nameless countries mean little.

Each distinct approach to reading a map emphasizes a different aspect of its information. Most maps tell us about geographic location; their primary dimension is spatial, not temporal. How we look at a map depends on

Military operations depend on knowledge of topography, and military maps were among the first to represent terrain schematically. This 1676 map of Brest in 1:886 scale shows the network of the town's surrounding roads—leaving them secretively unnamed—as well as fortifications, fields, and waterways.

what knowledge we expect it to supply; how we interpret its signs depends on how those signs are presented, and with what intent. Maps are therefore much more subjective than they may at first appear.

Image-maps and instrument-maps

A map converts a three-dimensional landscape to an abstract, two-dimensional form and freezes it at a moment in time. Maps, like landscape paintings, often display towns and mountains, forests and rivers, yet the two forms of image are fundamentally unalike. Early maps attempted to reproduce a landscape's treatment of space, with recession into depth and buildings and mountains presented as if at eye-level, planted firmly on the ground. Such maps

"He doth smile his face into more lines than are in the new map with the augmentation of the Indies."

William Shakespeare,
Twelfth Night,
III, ii, 1601

attempted to communicate both political facts, such as the relationship of one city to another, and a realistic picture of the world.

At the end of the 13th century nautical maps called portulans appeared in Europe. These conveyed specific navigational information and rendered the physical world schematically, removing unnecessary details. They showed coastlines, ports, prevailing winds, currents, and other important data in the clearest way possible. As cartography developed over the next two or three centuries, these were no longer image-maps, but rather instrument-maps, striving for precision and usefulness.

Some navigational maps were structured on networks of lines branching out from a series of compass roses, placed at certain latitudes and meridians. A compass rose

Here be dragons

Early European maps left unexplored territories a mysterious and evocative blank. Unfamiliar seas were decorated with vivid monsters. Left: this beast was painted in 1583, the twilight of that era, when maps represented the threshold between the unknown and the knowable.

is a sign symbolizing the four cardinal compass points, north, south, east, and west, and the secondary and tertiary directions. Direction is a key navigational (and cartographic) element; in old maps the compass points were often referred to as winds (north wind, south wind, and so on). In many portulans the lines for the four main winds are in black, the half winds in red, and the quarter winds in green. Another group of prominent signs are the flags, pennants, or blazons indicating the positions of towns and ports. The Portuguese, Spanish, and Genovese explorers of the 16th century used maps to illustrate and record the routes of the great discoveries.

B elow left: in this detail of the c.1550 world map by the Frenchman Pierre Desceliers (1487–1553) wilderness is represented by wild animals and mountainous regions are depicted as tiny individual mountain landscapes with sprouting trees; there is no attempt at drawing to scale.

Navigators and their map makers sometimes used secret codes and kept their maps hidden and guarded, for new trade routes were a valuable asset to a nation, representing access to all the wealth of the Indies, the East, and the New World.

The invention of the topographic map

Between the 14th and 17th centuries European map making developed steadily, especially in Flanders and Holland. Cartographers such as the Fleming Gerard Mercator (1512–94) published new maps and globes using the best printing methods, the latest research of explorers, the most precise drafting instruments, and the most accurate measurements of astronomers. The process of measuring distance and position on the curved surface of the terrestrial globe by triangulation permitted flat paper maps to represent curved surfaces without undue distortions.

Nautical maps are guides to seafarers; global maps indicate national territories and political boundaries; but in the 18th century another kind of map came into being that told a citizen what sort of place he or she lived in.

A case in point is the detailed topographical map of France drafted in the early 1700s by the Cassinis, a

The great Cassini survey map of France (below, a detail), composed between 1733 and 1784, uses a very different symbolism to render the idea of terrain: forests are stylized clusters of trees, mountains are topographically rendered; all is seen from a single, unified viewpoint above the earth.

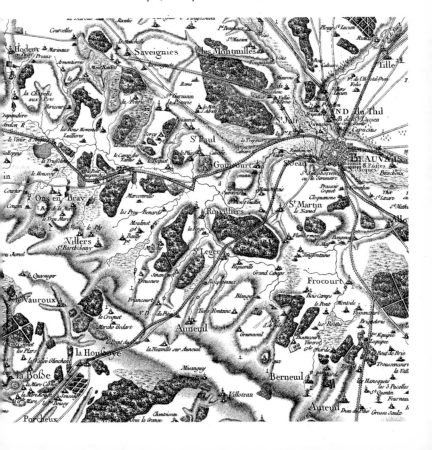

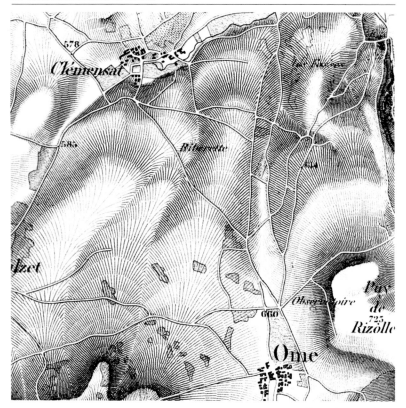

family of French astronomers, surveyors, and cartographers. France at this time was essentially a rural country; the abundant, varied signs on the Cassini map are drawn realistically to represent categories of natural features—woodland, heath, swamp, hills—as well as various types of paved and unpaved roads. Decorative flourishes such as cartouches, sea monsters, and compass roses have virtually disappeared. As a representation of France it is remarkably accurate, but it is not especially useful in telling us how to get from one place to another.

Map signs evolved into semiotic conventions as a by-product of a multitude of scientific and technical developments. An example of such transformation may

Over time, certain conventions in the signs used in maps were adapted internationally. The measurement of land elevations and other altitudes from a zero point at sea level was one of the most important of these.

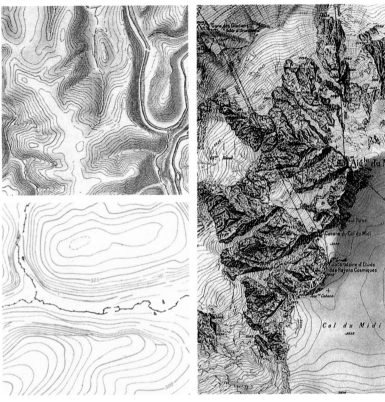

be seen in the signs that represent terrain topographically. Traditionally, mountains were indicated on maps by the small figure of a mountain in profile; on the Cassini map, however, they are depicted in bird's-eye view, as are all aspects of the land mass. Hachures (fine parallel hatch-marks) appear around the edges of each salient to indicate gradient; tighter hachures signify a steep incline, and high mountains are shaded.

The signs on topographic maps represent concrete realities

When maps began to describe topography, they faced a new challenge. Nautical maps use contour lines to represent the ocean depths, a sign system that is both

"It would be very advantageous if maps could show the elevations of all their elements, and indicate the distances between them on a horizontal plane…. What good is it to know that here is one mountain, there another, if I am given no indication of their dimensions, no information regarding their heights?"

Anonymous, 1802

easy to read and straightforward to render. It is relatively simple to measure the depth of a body of water, taking the flat surface of the water as a zero point.

The depiction of three-dimensional land on a flat piece of paper is quite another story, since there is no single zero point on the ground at which to place the first contour line as a base. Many maps nonetheless use a contour-line system for land forms like that used for water. An innovative map of 1881 uses a different approach: a system of hachures of carefully graduated lengths represents relief by a sort of optical illusion. Hachures are of different lengths as well, and the spacing between lines is calculated precisely. Contours are suggested by the position, length, and spacing of the hachures.

Refined printing methods allow modern relief maps to use color to great effect. Aerial and satellite photography and computer imaging have also contributed to greater precision in the sign systems of maps. And cartographers may even use shaped paper or thin molded plastic to create maps in which contours are represented by literal relief—a miniaturization of the actual terrain, which may not be a sign at all.

A tourist map of the Hawaiian Islands makes a point of illustrating their ecology and renders them in a naturalistic, decorative manner, with lots of bright colors. The signs in such a map should not be too abstract to be immediately decodable.

THE ISLANDS OF HAWAII

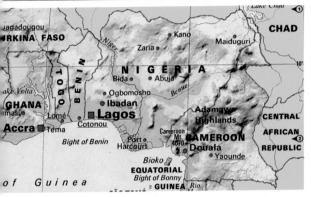

The cartographer is a wellspring of signs

The modern cartographer is almost a philosopher: both are concerned with the representation and interpretation of reality, its metaphors, and its abstractions. The map maker attempts to follow reality as closely as possible, avoiding ambiguities and false signals—though as with any practice that abstracts precise information from a wealth of data, interpretive biases are inevitable in maps.

The science that explores these problems is called semiology, or sign theory, the study of the graphic and symbolic use of signs. It distinguishes two coexisting semiotic categories: abstract signs, which bear no proportional or referential relationship to the things they represent, and representational signs, which portray the realities depicted on the map in a relatively proportional or literal manner. An example of the first category is the round dot that may indicate a town on a road map, without reference to the actual shape, extent, or population density of the site. An example of the second sort is the highly representational blue line that may indicate a river on a different sort of map, reproducing all its most minute bends and turns, and widening realistically at the mouth.

Topographic maps tend to prefer the latter sort of sign, while demographic or economic maps often favor the more iconic symbols. Both kinds of signs have their merits and shortcomings, and it is

The key, or legend, on a map defines many of its graphic conventions. In theory it should explain all of them, but in practice it is never exhaustive. Certain signs are sufficiently clear not to require translation. Almost never, for example, is there an explicit explanation of the symbols for rivers (wavy blue lines) or coastlines (lines that separate blue areas from areas of other colors). The cartographer assumes that some essential characteristics of his or her system of representation will be universally understood.

He had bought a large
     map, representing
     the sea,
   Without the least
     vestige of land:
And the crew were much
     pleased when they
     found it to be
   A map they could
     all understand.

"What's the good of
     Mercator's North
     Poles and Equators,
   Tropics, Zones and
     Meridian Lines?"
So the Bellman would
     cry: and the crew
     would reply
   They are merely
     conventional signs!"
       Lewis Carroll,
   The Hunting of the Snark,
       1876

The evolution of cartographic symbols

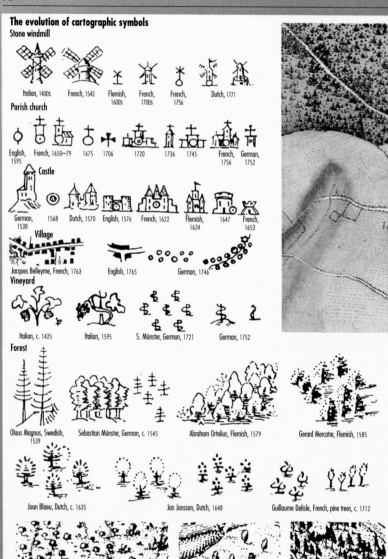

Stone windmill

Italian, 1400s | French, 1543 | Flemish, 1600s | French, 1700s | French, 1756 | Dutch, 1771

Parish church

English, 1595 | French, 1650–79 | 1675 | 1706 | 1720 | 1736 | 1745 | French, 1756 | German, 1752

Castle

German, 1538 | 1568 | Dutch, 1570 | English, 1576 | French, 1622 | Flemish, 1634 | 1647 | French, 1653

Village

Jacques Belleyme, French, 1763 | English, 1765 | German, 1746

Vineyard

Italian, c. 1425 | Italian, 1595 | S. Münster, German, 1721 | German, 1752

Forest

Olaus Magnus, Swedish, 1539 | Sebastian Münster, German, c. 1545 | Abraham Ortelius, Flemish, 1579 | Gerard Mercator, Flemish, 1585

Joan Blaeu, Dutch, c. 1635 | Jan Jansson, Dutch, 1648 | Guillaume Delisle, French, pine trees, c. 1712

chestnuts | deciduous trees | poplars | pines

All Jacques Belleyme, French, 1763

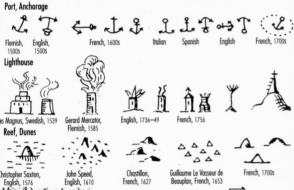

The language of geographers

Place icons have certain common characteristics. Such signs were at first figurative drawings, and attempted merely to represent objects, but gradually more schematic images evolved. The adoption of engraving for maps encouraged this process of increasing abstraction and generalization; realistic details were eliminated and eventually the literal image was replaced by a conventional sign. Nevertheless, map makers did attempt to retain the evocative power of their figures. Well-designed map signs are clear and speak for themselves. Though cartographers continued to create new signs based on the figurative tradition until the late 18th century, by the end of the 17th century a new approach had emerged, in which overhead views were favored and geometric signs were substituted for drawn signs.

Adapted from
François de Dainville,
Le Langage des géographes
(*The Language of
Geographers*), 1964,
pp. 324–29

Left and opposite: icons from old maps, collected and compared by François de Dainville in his study; above: detail of a 17th-century map of a French village surrounded by forests and cultivated fields.

Port, Anchorage

Flemish, 1500s   English, 1500s   French, 1600s   Italian   Spanish   English   French, 1700s

Lighthouse

...us Magnus, Swedish, 1539   Gerard Mercator, Flemish, 1585   English, 1736–49   French, 1756

Reef, Dunes

...hristopher Saxton, English, 1576   John Speed, English, 1610   Chastillon, French, 1627   Guillaume Le Vasseur de Beauplan, French, 1653   French, 1700s

...ques Cassini, French, 1756   Jacobus van Deventer, Dutch, 1556,   Nicolas de Nicolay, French, 1558   Olaus Magnus, Swedish, 1539

The cartographic legend

Triangulation points ....

Christian church, chapel, cemetery ....

Temple, chapel, tomb, cemetery ....

Islamic mosque (large), mosque (small), tomb, cemetery ....

Tower (two types), windmill .... Tr Tr Chem.

Monument, archaeological site, ruins.............................. Mon.

Kiosk, lookout point, campsite..

Athletic field, tennis court, mountain lodge .... E Ǝ

Excursion route.. GR R1

Provincial capital.. PF

Border and capital of an administrative district .... SP

Border and capital of an administrative subdistrict .... CT

Border and capital of a parish.. C

Topographic features: water level, dip, embankment ....

Tree, forest, grove..

Railway with straight tracks, railway siding ....

Disused railroad tracks, abandoned railroad tracks.............

Disused railroad tracks with tunnel ....

Cog railway, funicular railway ....

Divided roadway..

Three-lane roadway ....

Two-lane roadway ....

Narrow two-lane roadway ....

Narrow road ....

Main road, secondary road ....

Road label..

Narrow road, regularly maintained; narrow road, infrequently maintained...............

Forest track, service track...

Abandoned road, road under construction ....

Road with short tunnel, road with long tunnel...................

Main

Secondary

N 2   D 10

Deciduous forest

Coniferous forest

Mixed deciduous/
coniferous forest

Thinly planted woods

Sugarcane

Orchard

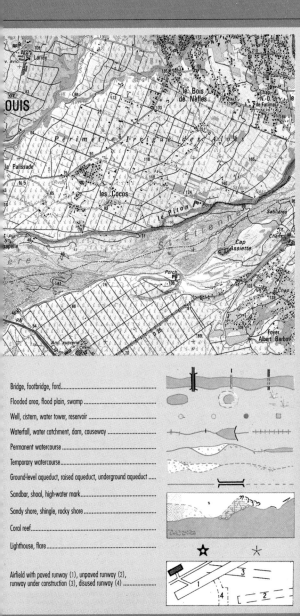

Bridge, footbridge, ford...

Flooded area, flood plain, swamp ....

Well, cistern, water tower, reservoir ....

Waterfall, water catchment, dam, causeway ....

Permanent watercourse ....

Temporary watercourse...

Ground-level aqueduct, raised aqueduct, underground aqueduct .....

Sandbar, shoal, high-water mark...

Sandy shore, shingle, rocky shore...

Coral reef...

Lighthouse, flare...

Airfield with paved runway (1), unpaved runway (2),
runway under construction (3), disused runway (4) ....

The cartographic legend translates symbols

A map legend is usually a small rectangle set discreetly in the corner of the page, within which most of the symbols used in the map are reproduced and explained—that is, translated into words. Symbols are listed in an orderly way, grouped according to type. The legend is far more important than its small size indicates and indeed is one of the most subtle and revealing components of a map. It represents the conversion of topographic and symbolic information into narrative. Far left: the legend we see here is extremely detailed. It belongs to a modern topographic map (of which we see only a small detail, above left) of the Île de la Réunion, an island off the east coast of Africa. Drawn in 1:25,000 scale by the French Institut National Géographique, it is intended for the general public. Note that the legend groups symbols by categories—religious sites, types of terrain, roads and railways, and so forth—and includes both man-made structures and natural features. This legend itself thus constitutes an extraordinary repertory of signs.

The portrait of a coast

Steep coastline

Sandy coast

High-water mark

Low-water mark
(hydrographic zero point)

Shoal

Sand and mud

LEVEL LINES

Well-defined   Poorly defined

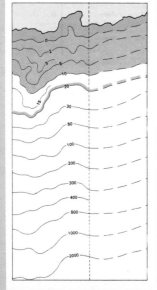

TERRAIN

Contour (altitude) lines

Forest

Swamp

DANGERS

Exposed rocks

Partially exposed rocks

Submerged rocks

Isolated submerged shoal

PORTS

⊖   Fishing port

⚓   Recreational port

⚓   Anchorage

🦅   Nature preserve

Mooring and fishing
prohibited

Mooring post

Bollard

Crane

Small post, pillar

Stairway

Quarantine office

Port station

Customs post

BUILDINGS

✚   Ch •   Church

† Cross

🏛 ⊙ Tr   Tower

✕   Windmill

🜨   Wind engine

🏛 ⊙ Water Tr   Water tower

🏛 ⊙ Mon   Monument

✉   Post office

⊕   Hospital

Town

Building

Fortification

Battery, blockhouse, small f

Creating a systematic landscape

Symbols are sited on a map according to a strict rule: each must be placed at the exact point on the map that corresponds to the position of the object on the ground. The map's grid system and plane coordinates (such as latitude and longitude lines) impose order and structure.

The legend organizes the same information according to an inverse rule: the signs are detached from their locations and arranged in columns, together with corresponding narrative definitions. This schematic format imposes a hierarchy of importance on the various signs—although the map maker, like a landscape artist, may not think of the terrain in such terms. A map is a collection of individual features; a legend is a collection of groups and subgroups. The apparatus of a map—legend, symbols, icons, labels, grid—converts its basic material into a formal construct. The legend has its own geometry; the grouping of elements follows its own rules, which are not those of the map, do not exist on the map itself, and introduce a supplementary grammar into the map's semiologic system. Left and above: legend and detail of a modern maritime map of the coast of Morbihan, in France.

NAVIGATIONAL BEACON SYSTEMS

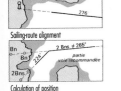

Sailing-route alignment

Calculation of position

Warning-light alignment

Lighthouse sector perimeters, indicating recommended shipping routes

LIGHTHOUSES AND SIGNAL LIGHTS

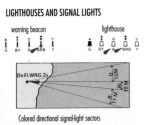

warning beacon

lighthouse

Colored directional signal-light sectors

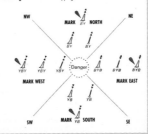

MARK NORTH
MARK WEST
MARK EAST
MARK SOUTH
Danger

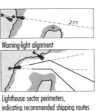

commonplace for maps to rely on both, as well as on supplementary written labels or text captions: on a political map, for example, the population of a city may be denoted in a number placed nearby; on a topographic map, such a number may signify feet above sea level. These written labels have their own semiotic tricks: a small town may be named in small type, while a large metropolis is labeled in boldface. Put another way, the visual attributes of signs at times contaminate words,

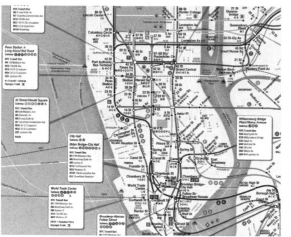

S cientific cartography began in the ancient world with astronomy. It developed along with that discipline and benefited from inventions in mathematics, such as trigonometric triangulation, draftsmanship, printing, and aerial photogrammetry. Computer imaging offers new levels of accuracy and efficiency, especially in the area of modeling. Above: a computer-generated diagram of Mont Blanc, in the Alps.

numbers, and letters, which thus become units in a graphic code.

The world represented by signs

Maps draw upon the signs used by researchers and technicians of all disciplines. Computers are especially prolific creators of synthetic images and signs of all types, as is television—from the curves representing the daily fate of the stock market to the graphic bars reporting election results or changes in the cancer rate to the pie chart that displays percentages of unemployment among different age groups. A diagram is a map not of a place

L eft: detail of a 1998 map of the New York City underground subway system, represented as a flowing tangle of colored lines.

but of a concept. It is a graphic, schematic description of a phenomenon, or of the correlation of several factors, or of the relationship of parts to a whole. The permutations of such maps, the variations in their forms and purposes, are infinite.

Sign systems are designed for clarity and therefore are often geometric and formal, yet the semiotic origins of even the most abstract maps may borrow from nature: a graphic that depicts a public-transportation network looks like a spiderweb; a family genealogy is drawn in the form of a many-branched tree.

Maps are not only useful, they are often beautiful, and the best cartographers take aesthetic issues into account in their designs. Below: a contemporary diagram of a telephonic network in the United States, rendered in glittering lights.

Bottom: a 1994 map of the world in which nations are scaled to

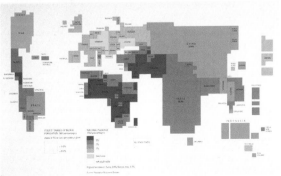

represent not geographic forms, but proportional share of the world's population. The physical position of each state and the general silhouette of the continents have been retained. Colors indicate rates of population increase or decline. Such schematic maps as this expose the ways in which every map emphasizes certain facts and suppresses others.

Since early antiquity people have oriented themselves by natural signs: sailors navigated by constellations, the Magi followed a star. When these proved insufficient, we invented others, some of which are culturally specific. Invented signs were added to the natural ones.

CHAPTER 5
ROAD SIGNS

Left: a storm-tossed ship homes to the signal of a lighthouse; right: Venus, the Morning Star, appears in the eastern sky at dawn and the western sky at dusk and has long been a road sign for voyagers. For thousands of years the sun, moon, and stars guided travelers; the map of the sky still offers a vast reservoir of reference points for those lost and wandering the earth.

When the first railroad appeared in England at the beginning of the 19th century, the art of signaling was born. This was a system of signs used both to indicate direction and to ensure the safety of those who worked with these fire-breathing iron monsters.

Railroad signaling is a simple binary system of warning signs and go-ahead signs

England had one of the earliest extensive railway networks in the world. Once switches were installed, a signal system became essential for safety. Until the 1840s English trains were guided by guards posted on station platforms, at junctions, and at level crossings. They controlled the passage of trains, waving them through or giving them the order to stop, using signal flags by day and lanterns by night. There were three rudimentary signs: a flag or lamp covering the agent's body meant that the way was clear; a raised flag was a caution sign; a lowered flag alerted the conductor and engineer of the locomotive to a defect in the tracks.

This type of signaling is based on the principle of binary opposition, which is succinct, simple, and clear. In the language of train signals signs indicating permission

Below: in the early years of the 20th century railroad signaling was still rudimentary. Trains were much less frequent and slower than they are today and tracks were still thought of as literal roads, controlled manually by switchmen and railwaymen—or, as here, women. Opposite above: children too were employed to carry signals on train lines; opposite below: at night, or when the weather turned harsh, train engineers relied heavily upon light signals to avoid a crash.

and those indicating warning are visibly oppo-site to one another. These signs establish an elementary, rapid form of communication between the stationary signer and the individual operating a train in motion.

Gradually, the hand-held flag and lantern were replaced by mechanical-arm semaphores.

Railway signals evolved as speed and traffic increased

To make this system efficient, railway lines were divided into sectors. A semaphore was placed at the beginning and end of each section of rail. This principle, still used in places today, permitted only one train at a time to enter a sector. Hence, an interval of space between two successive trains also implied an interval of time. The system

improved further when signals and switches could be engaged at the same time.

In 1852 an English process was perfected that eventually made a dramatic difference to the efficiency and security of the railways. A switch mechanism was placed inside the rails at the entrance and exit of each sector; when a train passed it was lowered to close an electric circuit, setting off a visual signal at the signal-box. This was the ancestor of the famous automatic brake, thanks to which modern trains trip their own signals, which turn red as they pass.

Road signs have two key features: the configuration of the network to which they belong and the freedom of its users to move about in it

For much of history road signs consisted mainly of milestones and signposts directing travelers to towns. The ancient Romans, who were masterful road builders, had both. But it was only with the invention of the internal combustion engine in the 19th century that the need arose for a more sophisticated system. Speed was the cause: in 1894 the median speed in the automobile race from Paris to Rouen was nearly 12½ miles (21 kilometers) per hour; in 1901, on the Paris-to-Berlin course, it was 43½ miles (74 kilometers) per hour. Thereafter car speeds continued to increase steadily. Early cars were unreliable and their drivers not always skilled. By the 1890s people had begun to have serious road accidents, and governments turned their attention to instituting licensing laws and rules of the road.

Road signs were born at this time. With them came the notion that to commit a traffic infraction was a crime and could expose the culprit to arrest. As the automobile

The semaphore system utilized a simple mechanical device. Left: a semaphore in operation; opposite above: a French level-crossing sign; when the red light is lit, the reader of the sign need not know French to understand that it is appropriate to stop; below: a Russian train moving through fog pauses at a semaphore with lowered arms, obeying the signal to *wait*.

industry grew, networks of roads were expanded; indeed, in much of Europe and the United States road systems and rail systems developed almost together and often literally intersected, while horse-drawn vehicles remained a common presence—not to mention pedestrians, farm animals, bicyclists, and other road users. To regulate all this new traffic not only were road signs needed, but an integrated design program that would work internationally and be instantly readable at almost any speed. One of the first modern road-sign systems to take account of the needs of automobile drivers was that produced in 1895 by the Italian Touring Club, which also produced road maps. In 1900 an international congress was convened in Paris to establish a

Traffic lights are an important element in road signage, regulating major intersections. Between the green go light and the red stoplight is the yellow caution light, as well as the blinking light that signifies "proceed with caution." Even on today's highly automated roads traffic police supplement lights with strictly codified gestures and blasts of a whistle. Left: a mid-century advertisement for cars glamorizes the bustling street.

Right: pedestrian crosswalks, sometimes called zebra crossings, are often designated by large striped bands painted on the road, in white or yellow, depending on the country. This crosswalk is in Japan. Far right: four road signs designed by the Italian Touring Club in 1908. From top: a directional sign indicates the distance to two towns near Venice, Treviso, and Roncade; a warning sign uses an abstract circle to signify "slow down"; another warning sign indicates a dangerous descent, or steep grade; and a broken arrow indicates an interrupted road ahead. Notwithstanding their typographic elegance, these signs are less than fully effective. Note that all are in black and

standardized international system; among the first signs chosen then were those warning of a BUMP, CURVE, INTERSECTION, and RAILROAD CROSSING.

Signs understood worldwide and at a single glance

Like most other sign systems, road signs are a mixture of abstract conventional symbols and stylized images that maintain at least a partial analogy to the things they designate. However, road signs present a number of graphic-design problems that distinguish them from the sets of signs that appear in public places such as railway stations or hospitals. They must be consistent and yet must address a wide variety of specific situations. Often several signs appear together, and their relative importance and distinct purposes must be instantly clear. Not only do they describe what features of the roadscape a traveler will find up ahead, they also explain the proper, legal behavior in force for each segment of the road network. They must serve equally well for the driver of a

white—presumably for legibility, but overlooking the potential power of color to convey meaning. The "dangerous descent" sign uses an abstract icon with great effect, but the meaning of the "slow down" circle is far less clear. Still, these early Italian designs were remarkably innovative and even stylish.

two-ton truck and a child on foot, walking a puppy on a leash. In addition to all this, they must function in a wide range of cultures whose basic assumptions about how to interpret icons, colors, and symbols may differ greatly. And their meaning must be accessible in the blink of an eye to a driver traveling at high speed.

The rules of the road are formulated in a code of signs that makes use of shape, color, and hieroglyphic marks to convey meaning. In the international road-sign system that is now common in much of the world a triangle indicates danger or warning (ROAD WORK AHEAD; YIELD);

a circular sign is a prohibition (DO NOT ENTER; NO PARKING); a rectangular sign bears a message of simple information. Colors too have fixed meanings: red = danger, yellow = caution, and so on.

These units of basic signification are combined to represent particular features, configurations, or circumstances of the road in a very formulaic manner. To them are added other, less rigidly stylized signs, which derive their meaning at least partly

from local context. Many of the principles on which modern road signs are based today were developed by Otto Neurath (1882–1945), a German philosopher and sociologist who studied graphic symbols in the 1920s. Like railway signs, road signs also use coded lights—blinking and of various colors—to indicate when to move or stop. However, the road network is essentially different from the railroad network in one respect: no mechanical system controls the actual motions of a vehicle.

In order to tell drivers not only about present conditions and rules of the road, but also what to expect in the immediate future, road signs employ a repertory of images that describe topography and other physical features: a dangerous turn, a

The international system of road signs is in wide use throughout the world and is beginning to be embraced in the United States, which long maintained its own designs. International road signs use abstract icons, figurative silhouettes, and purely conventional elements, such as color, to express a variety of ideas. This page, from top: *do not pass; no right turn, no left turn; stop ahead; railroad crossing; caution: animal crossing.*

In spite of the efforts toward international sign systems—from road signs to languages of the deaf—local and language-based signs remain common. Opposite, below left: a sign warning of a caribou crossing communicates well internationally; one does not really need the written explanation below the yellow diamond to grasp that large horned animals cross the road at this point. Note that the phrase "caribou crossing" has itself been rendered in a semi-iconic shorthand: XING.

hill, a bridge, a narrowing of the road, an intersection, an overpass or flyover. A second series of signs establishes the code of conduct: these are signs of restriction and limitation, such as of speed, parking, and passing, not to mention street direction. Road signs often work in sets: a warning of a dangerous curve may be paired with one forbidding passing on the curve; a sign signaling entrance into a populated area is accompanied by one limiting speed. These things seem obvious—even self-evident, but they are part of a carefully constructed complex of abstract symbols.

Maritime signaling is the most ancient: lighthouses and flags are ancestral languages

The Pharos, or Lighthouse, of Alexandria, built on an islet in the harbor of that Egyptian coastal city in the 3d century BC, was one of the seven wonders of

Sometimes a sign symbol alone is not enough. Left: a conventional orange dot signifies a warning, and an arrow indicates where the danger lies, but this sign also adds specific information—"Danger, overhanging rocks, 50 meters ahead"—that fails to maintain the highest standards of communicability. Not only is important information in one language only, but to indicate the distance in meters assumes a knowledge of the metric system. The snow piled on the sign adds its own seasonal warning voice. Below: a simple directional arrow gains additional force when it is doubled; this pair of signs warns of a detour.

Fig.I. Niding

Fig.IV. Wipp-Feuer 1560.

Above left: a 19th-century publication from the port city of Trieste (now in Italy) explains maritime flag signals, fancifully placing several atop a lighthouse, as if they were signal beacons.

the ancient world. It was an immense tower with a signal fire at the summit, whose light was reflected far out to sea by a huge burnished metal mirror. Alexandrian mariners quartering the Mediterranean could find their home port while still miles away. Though destroyed in an earthquake long ago, it is the most ancient known maritime signal and has given its name to later light towers used to guide and warn ships. A signal fixed at one point on land, a lighthouse may mark the entrance to a port, the proximity of an island or roadstead, or a perilous shoal or reef. Lighthouses indicating a nearby shore are generally the most powerful; lesser lighthouses aid navigation along shorelines; and a modest flare may

Fig. II. Djursten 1765.

Fig. III. Neufahrwasser 1758.

Fig. V. Isle of May 1635.

Fig. VI. Spurn-Point 1776.

Fig. VII. Cordouan.

serve the same purpose as a buoy, denoting the entrance to a port or navigable marked channel.

Yet far more ancient than the Alexandrian Lighthouse is the use of the maritime flag. Flags have identified and signaled boats for thousands of years. Ship's banners dating to the reign in the 12th century BC of the Egyptian pharaoh Ramesses II have been found in Egyptian tombs; the first sure traces of the use of maritime ensigns for signaling ship-to-ship or ship-to-shore date to the 9th century BC. Flags of different shapes and colors, or held in different positions, could convey messages as simple as a ship's nationality, or as complex as that its crew was stricken with illness.

In the Renaissance, the great age of sailing, a navy was the principal armed force of many nations. By the end of

The practice of signaling and guiding ships by means of onshore beacon lights is very ancient. Lighthouses and lanterns have indicated routes, safe havens, and dangers to boats ever since early antiquity. Above: an old color engraving illustrates a number of antique shipping beacons; some are hung in slings, so that they may be moved vertically or laterally to send a specific signal out to sea.

the 16th century the English, whose navy was beginning to command the world's seas, had developed an intricate flag system that distinguished the different components of the fleet with different colored flags, red, blue, and white.

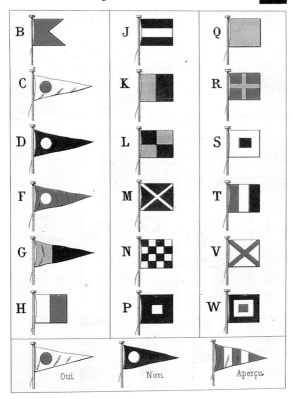

B
C
D
F
G
H
J
K
L
M
N
P
Q
R
S
T
V
W

Oui

Non

Aperçu.

The language of maritime flag signals uses flags of different shapes and colors held in different arm positions. Above and opposite page: a sailor uses flag signals to form the letters *Y, E, X.* Left: in some codes each flag corresponds to a letter of the alphabet, forming a sort of Morse code. Other flags represent whole words: the three at bottom signify "yes," "no," and "seen," or "sighted." These ingenious sign systems are now almost obsolete, since they depend on the relative proximity of sender to receiver and the unobstructed view of both. Electricity, wireless radio, radar, computers, and satellites have replaced them. Today, shipboard flags are more likely to be used for festive decorations and to indicate nationality.

Signs fixed in the ocean

A beacon is a maritime signal light that marks a sea route (usually coastal) and aids a navigator to avoid such dangers as submerged reefs or shallow channels. Like lighthouses, beacons are especially useful at night or in fog, when flags are ineffective. Being small and portable, these floating lights are often used to mark new dangers, such as a recent wreck not yet recorded on maritime maps.

The history of beaconing systems has certain similarities with that of railroad signaling: both developed rapidly and internationally. Until 1976 there were more than thirty different systems in the world. Since shipping is an international business, this created considerable confusion. A navigator who suddenly saw a nearby beacon and was unable to interpret its meaning with confidence was in danger. The rules regarding the placement of beacons and flares were inconsistent—and consistency, as we have seen, is one of the hallmarks of a good sign system. In some countries beacons were placed

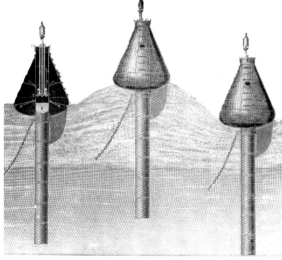

L eft: whistling buoys are another form of maritime signal. A buoy is moored to a shoal, wreck, or other danger-ous submerged object; the movement of the waves activates a system of piston-whistles within it, so that it emits a steady noise.

laterally, so that the navigator was to steer between pairs of flares; others adopted the system of cardinal marks, in which a danger was indicated by one or more beacons that oriented it to a cardinal point of the compass. For many years the seas of the world were divided into those that used System A (Europe, Africa, and Australia), in which, for example, a red beacon indicated the port side of a channel; and seas using System B (North and South America and the Pacific Rim countries), which used the same color to indicate the starboard side of a channel. It was not until 1980 that a fully international system of beaconing was established. This story suggests the extent to which signs and their meanings depend on conventions and hence on a perfectly arbitrary code.

Boats themselves carry signs

Not only have ships traditionally depended on buoys, beacons, shore lights, and lighthouses, but they have their own rigorous light codes and flag languages. For example, shipboard lights distinguish between a sailboat and a motorboat. Sailboats have a white light atop the tallest mast; depending on their tonnage they may also display other lights: a red running light on the port side and a green one on the starboard side.

In beacon System A, beacons are placed in lateral pairs; the portside one is cylindrical and red (above) and the starboard one (opposite) is conical and green.

Altogether, sailing signals use a relatively small number of signs: like the pennants and triangular flags used by day, lights, flares, and rockets convey messages by color and position, as well as by rhythmic blinking (as in Morse code). Bells, whistles, compressed-air sirens, foghorns, and electromagnetic vibrators are sound-based signal devices often used in fog. As a whole, the maritime system is more coherent than the code of the road, but less sophisticated than railway signaling. It is notable for its economy and efficiency.

Radio signals

Modern travel and shipping—whether by road, sea, or air—require security, speed, and precision. So do modern military and scientific endeavors, and other forms of human commerce and interaction. The development of high-frequency radio technology during World War II (1939) altered the world of signal communications dramatically, introducing radar, sonar, and other wireless transmitting and receiving devices. Radar, an acronym for RAdio Detecting And Ranging, is used to detect distant objects, often hidden or beyond the range of visibility. A transmitter emits high-frequency electromagnetic (radio) waves (either broadcast or directionally focused); when these strike the target object the signal is reflected, forming an "image"; a radar receiver reads and analyzes the reflected signals to identify the nature and location of the object. At various points in this process the information

being transmitted and received may be converted into codes, both to convey it more efficiently and to conceal it.

Other related signal systems include sonar, which sends and receives ultrasonic signals under water, and Magnetic Resonance Imaging, or MRI, which is used in medicine to detect foreign bodies in organic tissue. Radio imaging systems have grown extremely precise and fast and can be used to protect and guide aircraft, shield a territory from the approach of a missile, find a sunken treasure in the depths of the ocean, or discover a tumor in the brain.

B elow: a small sailboat passes between two navigation beacons, as a big ocean liner waits.

Air and space: to Jupiter and beyond

Airplane pilots and navigators, like those on ships, communicate both by voice, over a radio, and by conventionalized international signals. Aviation signaling uses a network of signs that draws some elements from the road system (painted marks on runways, hand gestures by ground traffic controllers) and others from the maritime tradition (radar instruments and those that measure altitude, direction, and wind speed, as well as specialized maps and commands from the control tower). Runways are striped with take-off and landing guides, and with marks, in tenths of degrees, that indicate their orientation with respect to magnetic north.

Computers and satellite technology have advanced the speed and precision of all these signal systems, and created others. At one end of the range we find that even the most commonplace communications of the Internet and cyberspace are rapidly developing their own language codes, modes of expression, visual symbols, and convenient shorthand

Above: in the early days of flight, night landings at airfields were very hazardous. The pilot was guided by light beacons. Today, airports are lit by white ground lights that mark the edges of the runway and red and white lights that guide the plane. The pilot also uses radar, radio, and voice commands from the control tower.

Below: an arrow marks the landing runway at a modern airport.

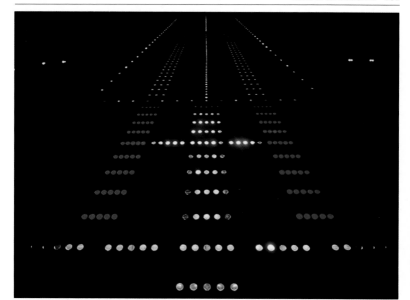

vocabularies, and that many of these are becoming internationally accepted across language borders. At the other end, research and applied astronomy have long been the greatest innovators in the use and design of radio-signal systems. At radio-telescope sites around the world the SETI (Search for Extraterrestrial Intelligence) Project scans the galaxies for hints of radio code—electromagnetic microwave signals—emanating from some distant world.

But in any case, to read and use the signal systems of road, sea, air, and space we still rely on the eye to see the signs, the ear to hear them, and the mind to understand them: our greatest sign skills are discernment, observation, interpretation, and experience.

For all our navigating, in our real or imaginary journeys, we will long continue to use the signs that aided the first travelers to find their bearings: the sun, the moon, and the stars.

To find the right angle for descent onto the runway, a pilot is guided by clusters of ground lights, which function as beacons. These appear in a set order: white-over-white lights mean that the airplane is too high; red-over-red warn that it is too low; white-over-red signify that the plane is in correct alignment to land. Below: a runway technician guides a pilot into a docking position using signal paddles.

Ｗe invent new signs and icons every day. What happens to those created over thousands of years of human civilization? Some are lost, abandoned to oblivion, while others endure—retaining or altering their meaning, becoming less or more important to us. Time tests a sign's capacity to anchor itself in the history of a people, or to transcend it and inscribe itself in our collective memory. Time turns signs into symbols.

CHAPTER 6
FROM SIGN TO SYMBOL

Signs are sometimes direct allegories. Left: in this Netherlandish Renaissance painting by Jan Provoost, *Sacred Allegory,* c. 1500, the Eye, the Mystical Lamb, and the Dove are figures of the Christian Trinity: Father, Son, and Holy Spirit. Christ and the Virgin are witnesses to this apparition. Right: the balance, placed within the constellation of Libra (the Scales) in this medieval miniature, is an allegory of Justice.

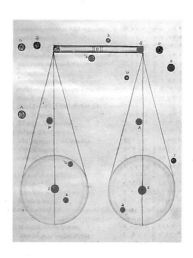

Sign systems are codes organized empirically, for specific ends. For example, map-making signs function well only in the context of maps; road signs regulate traffic, but are useless on the open ocean. Sign codes are not interchangeable, though one code may borrow from another, and some famous signs have a history of changing meanings.

Families of signs

In addition to belonging to a sign system, some signs also belong to family groups, which have their own history. The family of directional pictograms, for example, is universal and spans the ages. From the small black footprints traced on ancient Aztec codices to the Victorian pointing hand, to the modern directional arrow, in all its graphic forms, this is one of the oldest families of signs in the world.

Families of signs are grouped by meaning or usage. From time immemorial humankind has expressed basic sentiments with pictograms: the crying eye signified sorrow in ancient Egyptian hieroglyphics and seems to have had the same meaning in pre-Columbian cave paintings of North America, on the other side of the globe. Similarly universal is the unforgettable family of signs representing fear, danger, or forewarning, from the pictogram of the death's head on pirate flags and bottles of poison to the symbol of the lightning bolt posted on high-voltage electrical towers. Note that a sign with a rich and varied history, such as the skull, may turn up in many families; that is, it has more than

Three versions of the directional sign range from full pictorial representation to pure sign. Above: one of the three Magi points to the guiding Star of Bethlehem; left: a Victorian typographic hand, with pointing index finger; below: the arrow, stylized graphic descendant of two concrete objects, hand and weapon.

The death's head is a symbolic sign whose message varies according to its context. Above: the skulls with crossed shinbones on this nautical flag indicate a pirate ship, with fearsome death aboard. Center: this death's head belongs to a 17th-century *Vanitas* image, a metaphysical symbol reminding the viewer to meditate on the lines from Ecclesiastes, "Vanity of vanities; all is vanity"; life and its splendors end in death. Below: inscribed in a triangle, signifying *caution,* this modern skull-and-crossbones pictogram tells us of a danger that is potentially lethal. In all three cases, the sign functions as symbol.

one meaning, depending on the context, culture, and time in which it appears. The skull as a secular symbol may warn of danger, or pose a threat; in Christian iconography it may be a *memento mori,* a pious reminder to meditate on the transience of the world, or a symbol of penitence. In Icelandic lore it refers to the

vault of heaven. In alchemy, Freemasonry, and some forms of Buddhist symbolism it may represent the contrary idea, referring to reincarnation.

Words describe and interpret signs, but cannot substitute for them

The sign, like the written word, is a container and transmitter of meaning. But the pictograph, the bodily gesture, and the drawn icon possess an irreducible economy of expression, an unmistakable abbreviation of certain

Clear and immediate, economical and unambiguous, the sign image has endured through the ages as a mode of communication; from ♥ to ⚡ to ♻ to ✉ to ⬆, we understand the signs of our times.

processes of communication, that words cannot match. There is no gap between the sign image and its meaning, no pause for translation from word to idea. The image simulates the presence of the object or concept it represents, both communicating the idea of it and giving it form, invested with a symbolic charge.

By an ancient tradition royalty is often symbolized by a scepter or rod. The baton of the ruler, like the wand of the magician, represents the mystical, divine, or supernatural authority of the king. It is an old convention to represent justice with the figure of a blindfolded woman holding a balanced pair of scales—though the scales as an image of justice date to the ancient world. Love is associated with the sign of the heart, which is the organ that lies in the middle of the body, the center of life. The passing of time is symbolized by a sickle, the curved blade that culls the harvest, so that a new growth cycle may begin. A fir tree or an evergreen plant may symbolize immortality or renewal, as does the Christmas tree of northern tradition or the Celtic mistletoe.

Rites and customs may be seen as symbolic systems

The family of signs includes yet another category: rites and customs. The practice of symbolic rituals is apparently as old as civilization; evidence of such rites has been found at Paleolithic sites. In early cultures no distinction was drawn between the profane and sacred world. Some rituals that we maintain today have origins lost in the mists of the past. The memory of the sign is inherited, transmitted through generations, while the explanation of its meaning or

Below: in the allegory of the French Revolution, the figure of *Fraternité*, or brotherhood, holds a heart in one hand and shelters two children beneath her cloak, a black child and a white one, amicably embracing. Opposite: monks in a Renaissance miniature form a funeral procession. Here the color black is a sign of mourning. The symbolic meanings of colors are culturally determined; in China the color symbolizing mourning is white.

Iconography in paintings: the symbolism of hands

What are the visual symbols of marriage? Far left: *The Arnolfini Double Portrait*, by Jan van Eyck, 1434; near left: Vrancke van der Stockt, marriage scene, detail from the *Redemption* triptych, c. 1470. In medieval Christian art the symbolism of the couple focuses on the hands, in particular the right hand. In Van Eyck's painting the woman's hand rests in the man's, turned upward; in Van der Stockt's the two are clasped in a paired gesture beneath the blessing hands of the priest. This symbolism echoes the tradition that has the male suitor "ask for the hand" of his future wife, while she "gives him her hand in marriage." It is also the hand that wears a wedding ring, circular symbol of unity, faith, and perfection.

The Arnolfini Double Portrait celebrates the marriage of Giovanni Arnolfini and Giovanna Cenami and is laden with symbols relating to marriage: the little dog represents domestic fidelity; the crystal prayer beads hanging on the back wall suggest faith; near them, at center, is a convex mirror that may be understood as the benevolent, observing eye of God, watching over the couple.

The engagement ring

To become engaged means to promise one's faith in marriage. The engagement ring marks a bond freely entered into. In Lucas van Leyden's 16th-century portrait of an engaged couple the eyes as well as the hands are essential sign symbols. The man slips an engagement ring onto the woman's index finger (the ring finger is reserved, as its name indicates, for the wedding band), as the two gaze at one another. Rings were used as love and marriage tokens in ancient Rome, a practice that was adopted by early Christianity. Isidore of Seville (c. 560–636) wrote that a ring "was given by the spouser to the espoused whether for a sign of mutual fidelity or still more to join their hearts to this pledge."

Gestures and ceremonies

In the 19th century European engravings recorded ceremonies from other cultures seen as exotic. Far left: a Muslim marriage in Sumatra uses symbolic hand gestures, which indeed are still very common in wedding rituals the world over. Near left, above: among the Mandingo people of West Africa the bridegroom proposes marriage while kneeling before a priest, watched by the bride. Near left, below: in another Mandingo ceremony of the period a newborn child's name is made official with immersion in water—not unlike the Christian ceremony of baptism.

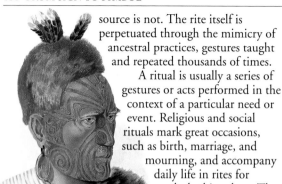

source is not. The rite itself is perpetuated through the mimicry of ancestral practices, gestures taught and repeated thousands of times.

A ritual is usually a series of gestures or acts performed in the context of a particular need or event. Religious and social rituals mark great occasions, such as birth, marriage, and mourning, and accompany daily life in rites for meals, bathing, love. The influential Swiss psychologist and philosopher Carl Gustav Jung (1875–1961) suggested that a rite is a message whose meaning escapes individual interpretation and takes root in the collective unconscious of society. A community practices a ritual to express its identity and to nurture its own memory; like other signs, then, a rite or ritual is concerned with recording and remembering, as well as communicating.

It is always easier to see the fixed, ritual nature of a tradition when it is not our own. The European and American folk tradition of touching iron or wood or tossing spilled salt over one shoulder for good luck may not seem like a ritual act to those who are familiar with it, whereas the rites of the indigenous peoples of non-western cultures may appear particularly vivid; thus, such "exotic" practices have often been studied by western anthropologists. One such is the practice of

Body decoration has complex social meanings—from the tattoo heart, inscribed MOTHER, on the biceps of an American sailor to the elaborate facial tattooing (left), representing spiritual armor, reserved for warriors among the Maori of New Zealand.

body painting or tattooing. The insightful French anthropologist Claude Lévi-Strauss (b. 1908) studied many distant cultures, and among other things was interested in these rituals of body decoration, which he understood as signs. He wrote: "Among the Maori, as among the natives of the Paraguayan border, facial and corporal decoration is executed in a semi-religious atmosphere.

Two Mojave Indians of California wear full body painting and tattoos in this illustration.

Tattooings are not only ornaments. As we already noted with respect to the [American] Northwest Coast (and the same thing may be said of New Zealand), they are not only emblems of nobility and symbols of rank in the social hierarchy; they are also messages fraught with spiritual and moral significance. The purpose of Maori tattooings is not only to imprint a drawing onto the flesh but also to stamp onto the mind all the traditions and philosophy of the group" (*Structural Anthropology I*, 1963, pp. 251–52). Inscribed in the history and culture of a people, a ritual bears profound symbolic value beneath its original practical function.

Such is the case of Freemasonry, a spiritual tradition that developed from the guilds of medieval Europe. A

Emblems in the heraldic style may represent a family, a guild, a political party. Above: a 15th-century Florentine majolica medallion, made for the guild of masons and carpenters, is decorated with an adz, surrounded by compass, right angle, trowel, and hammer and crossed chisels. Left: an 18th-century Masonic ceremonial apron is adorned with emblematic images of tools, columns, celestial bodies, trees, and a pyramid. These objects surround the Temple of Solomon, expressing moral values above and beyond their material use. A frequent symbol in Freemasonry is the triad: three trees, three openings in the temple, and three groups of three stars.

guild was similar to a union: a professional association of skilled craftsmen, with grades from apprentice to master and membership by invitation and initiation. In the 13th century masons were highly respected as the builders of the great cathedrals and were a free profession—that is, one not subject to feudal indenture. When, over several centuries, the Brotherhood of Freemasons grew into an esoteric fraternal organization, the tools and traditions of masons became the basis for a complex set of symbols and rites. Some became the secret signs by which Masons recognized one another; others were incorporated into Masonic rituals. The brotherhood is concerned with spiritual growth and humanistic ideals, which are

In Christian iconography the Lamb of God is a symbol of purity, innocence, and blessedness. This Renaissance majolica medallion of a haloed lamb carrying a pennant is the emblem of the powerful Florentine guild of wool merchants and cloth manufacturers. Here the Lamb indicates the organization's piety. The four fleurs-de-lys are Florentine lilies, emblems of the city. The wreath of fruits and vegetables suggests bounty and prosperity.

Left: Piero della Francesca's mid-15th-century fresco of *The Battle of Heraclius* from the cycle of *The Legend of the True Cross* displays heraldic banners of the contending armies, including the black eagle of the Holy Roman Empire and the gold lion of Venice—both contemporary, despite the painting's 7th-century subject.

Above and below: arms of the French town of Nancy, 19th century, and the Albret family, 16th century. Coats of arms are combinations of shapes, colors, and symbolic figures, used by groups of all sorts to identify themselves.

expressed in the symbolism of architecture and
the ancient tools of builders—hammer and
chisel, square and compasses, level,
plumb line, ruler, and carpenter's apron.
Each of these is used in Freemasonry's
elaborate symbolism, marking stages
in the initiate's spiritual
development.

Heraldry: the double function
of sign and symbol

Originally, in the 12th century, the
heraldic blazon was an insignia used to
identify helmeted knights and soldiers
in battles and tournaments. Over time, in
the course of the Middle Ages, armorial bearings
grew very elaborate and were used to identify
noble houses (often proclaiming the genealogical ties
among families), cities, guilds, confraternities, armies,
duchies, and nations.

Heraldry has its own highly formal symbolic and
pictographic language, in which all sorts of objects are
stylized and converted into signs, among them moons,

Animals are frequently
used as symbols.
Above: the Lamb of God
in a 19th-century gold and
silver embroidery; below:
the porcupine of Louis
XII, king of France, from
the royal château at Blois.

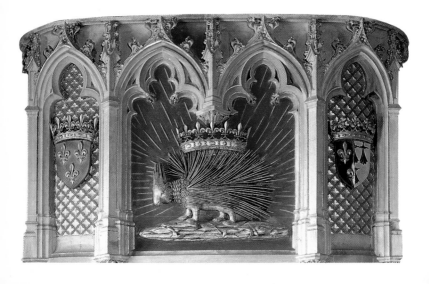

shells, buckles, chess pieces, crosses, and a plethora of beasts. Water is represented by wavy lines; a tower pierced by a door represents a town; immortality is depicted as a bird on a square. The medieval bestiaries are filled with the symbols used in blazons: the eagle (sometimes two-headed), lord of birds; the dove of the Holy Spirit; the salamander, unafraid of fire; the lion, king of beasts; various whales, dolphins, and fishes; and the mythological griffin, phoenix, dragon, basilisk, cockatrice, and unicorn. Every stripe, bar, and chequer on an armorial shield is formalized, as are the poses of animals. And all is described by a specialized vocabulary derived from Norman French.

Sign images make concrete the things of which language speaks

Sign images draw on, and refer to, our myriad acquired experiences and memories. They plunge us into a seething world of fragments and mental associations in which all things take on a symbolic value. This is one reason that religions use a great many symbols. Religious signs draw upon the customs and traditions in which we live and spark the emotions through a complex series of

The dove is one of Christianity's earliest symbols. This one is from the ancient Catacomb

of Priscilla in Rome. Below: according to legend the salamander was able to live in fire without burning. The great French Renaissance king François I adopted it as one of his emblems at Blois.

relations. They are the visual equivalents of metaphors and parables: images that represent very large ideas in small, compact packages.

Religious symbols express the ineffable in terms accessible to human sensibility

Most of the world's religions make use of visual symbols and icons. (Indeed, the word *icon* is derived from the classical Greek *eikon,* to resemble, and came to mean a sacred image in the Greek Christian church.) Christianity, with its powerful visual-art tradition, is notably rich in signs of varied sources and meanings. The symbolic representation of the Holy Spirit as a dove arose from the Christian fear of infringing divine law, for the direct representation of the image of God was forbidden. The white bird, wings outspread, is an image of the divine breath, the presence of God, hovering in transit between heaven and earth. Flowers acquire

Most religions imbue certain signs and gestures with symbolic value. Near right: the Catholic Pope Pius VI raises two fingers, tracing the sign of the Cross in a formal benediction. Below right: praying Muslims perform ritual genuflections, touching the ground with the forehead, as they turn toward the holy city of Mecca. Far right: like priests, kings often carry symbolic objects. Here, King Louis XI of France holds two scepters: one with the fleur-de-lys, symbol of the French monarchy, the other with the hand of Justice.

The sacerdotal robes of priests are often of specific colors or styles, or decorated in prescribed ways. Left: a druid priest in the white-and-gold robes of judgment, with a sacred snake and other ritual objects. Above, near right: the pope wears the papal tiara.

symbolic meanings: the white lily, with its ethereal perfume, is a symbol of virginity and radiance, midway between the spiritual and temporal world. Holly, evergreen in winter, with sharp thorns, and bearing red berries like drops of blood, is a symbol of Christ's Passion. And the Cross itself, is, of course, a symbol of suffering and redemption.

A prime emblem in Judaism is the six-pointed Star of David, also called the Seal of Solomon. Like many religious symbols it has accrued detailed and esoteric meanings. It is composed of two superimposed equilateral triangles —themselves laden with symbolism. It represents the interlacing of spirit and flesh, the active and passive principles. The Chinese symbol of *yin* and *yang* has some similarities: it is a circle divided in half by an *S*-shaped line the same length as half the circle's circumference; one

half is black, the other white: positive and negative, male and female, spiritual and material. Two opposites make a whole; the circle is the world, or the mind, or a complete being. These ideas are expressed in the Hindu fourfold mandala of the god Shiva: a square divided into four equal parts, the spatial symbol of the divine presence, a schematic image of the world, and the demarcation of the sacred precinct.

Indeed, in religious practice everything is symbol: the sacerdotal vestments; the decorations of church, temple, or mosque; the actions of the congregation; the gestures of the officiant during ceremonies; and the ceremonies themselves, all precisely structured in a closed, self-referential code.

The occult sciences are an immense reservoir of symbols

Alchemy, the zodiac, the Kabbalah, astrology, tarot cards, magic: the so-called occult sciences love symbols. In these disciplines the manipulation of the symbol is exceedingly delicate: the figure is not simply the sign of the thing or idea it represents, but its substitute. The goals of alchemy, forerunner of chemistry and pharmacology, are the Great Work (the transmutation of metals) and the search for the Philosopher's Stone and eternal youth. Alchemy uses an extremely complex language of graphic signs, representing metals, minerals, spices, planets, spirits, seasons, weights, and measures, whose value far surpasses a simple

reference to names. All of its esoteric operations are represented by these signs.

Astrology presents another repertory of signs, including the twelve figures of the zodiac, seasons, planets and moons, constellations, hours of day and night, days of the week, and signs for week, month, and year. With these intricate images as its tools, astrology explores the subjective ideas of destiny and fate.

Popular magic also possesses a system of coded symbols, drawn from a wide field of sources—Celtic and Christian, Egyptian and Asian. From time immemorial sages, sorcerers, and throwers of dice have learned the signs that kill and the signs that save, those that send a bolt of lightning or sudden illness, and those that promote fertility or make a loved one return.

The symbol spans history

Our modern pictograms often reuse and reinterpret ancient symbols, which are enriched by a long history. New symbols, on the other hand, generally do not accumulate layers of meaning so quickly, but limit themselves serving a useful purpose and expressing a meaning clearly. Two enduring signs provide interesting examples of

Left: the frontispiece to a 17th-century book of royal astrological charts combines a crown; the letter *L*, for King Louis; a centaur bestriding the letters SPQR, emblem of the Roman Empire to which France is heir; crossed palm fronds referring to Christian piety; astrological symbols; and the laurels of wisdom. Below: a witch casts a spell, using a beef heart.

Left: this pious monogram in the form of a cross comprises the Greek letters *XP* (*chi* and *rho*), the first two letters of the name *Christ;* and the first and last Greek letters, A and Ω, referring to the biblical text, "I am Alpha and Omega, the beginning and the ending, saith the Lord" (Rev. 1:8). Opposite: in the *Brera Altarpiece,* c. 1475, Piero della Francesca hangs an ostrich egg above the Madonna and Child. The egg is often a symbol of creation, fertility, unity, perfection, or totality.

the ways signs and symbols may acquire a history.

An international symbol of medicine is the caduceus, a rod entwined with two snakes. This image is antique: it is found engraved on a goblet from ancient Sumeria dating to 2600 BC and on stone tablets in India, and again in Greece, where it is the scepter of Hermes (Roman Mercury), the messenger god, and may symbolize equilibrium, fertility, the balance of opposing forces. As such it becomes the rod of Aesculapius, the god of medicine. Mercury himself later becomes the god of alchemy, representing the metal that changes form, thence his symbol is attached to the work of chemists and eventually, in our own day, physicians.

Another ancient symbol has had a less honorable fate. The swastika is one of the most venerable and widespread signs in the world, appearing in the arts of ancient civilizations from China to South America, from the Celts to the Etruscans to the Greeks. Medieval

Left: in a motif from a Persian seal-stamp, AD 226–641, a snake is twined about the World Tree. Below: twined snakes on a Celtic cross

and, below, on Hindu votive tablets.

Christianity used it as a sign for Christ: the world that revolves around a fixed center. In the same sense it is also the Buddha's Wheel of the Law. In many cultures it is the wheel of life, a figure of the cycles of the seasons, of regeneration and salvation. In the 9th century the emperor Charlemagne used the clockwise swastika as his royal symbol; in the 20th the genocidal German dictator Adolf Hitler, wishing to associate his totalitarian rule with such a potent history, took the counterclockwise swastika for his own symbol and tainted it forever.

In time, some symbols revert to being conventional signs

Some figures lose their symbolic force and become simple linguistic objects. Their past is forgotten, as are their often secret or obscure correspondences with the things, ideas, and concepts they once represented. In this sense, too, time transforms signs. Their figurative, representational character blurs and is conflated with their literal image; they become elements in an organized language. Thus the first Sumerian and Chinese pictograms and the first hieroglyphics of ancient Egypt became the signs of conventional systems of writing. Yet this transformation, which reduces symbols with multiple meanings to simple letters of an alphabet, is considered a mark of progress: it marks the moment in which humanity leaves the realm of myth and enters the dimension of space and history.

"The sign is a fracture that opens only into the image of another sign."
Roland Barthes,
Empire of Signs,
translated by
Richard Howard,
1970

B elow: a Japanese Buddhist statue of a monk meditating. Overleaf: the coat of arms of Bolivia and a 1960 map of the Mideast.

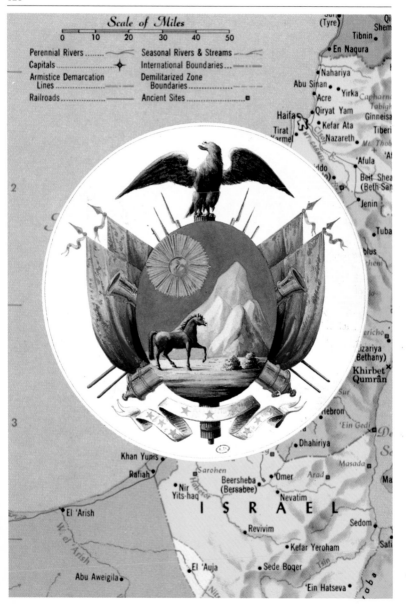

Scale of Miles

| 0 | 10 | 20 | 30 | 40 | 50 |

Perennial Rivers ....   Seasonal Rivers & Streams ....
Capitals .... ✦   International Boundaries....
Armistice Demarcation   Demilitarized Zone
    Lines ....   Boundaries ....
Railroads ....   Ancient Sites .... ▫

(Tyre)
Tibnin
En Naqura
Nahariya
Abu Sinan   Yirka
Acre
Qiryat Yam
Haifa   Kefar Ata   Ginneisa
Tirat   Nazareth
Karmel
'Afula
Beit Shea
(Beth-Sar
Jenin
Tuba
blus
Jericho
izariya
(Bethany)
Khirbet
Qumrân
Hebron
'Ein Gedi
Dhahiriya
Khan Yunis
Rafiah
Nir
Yits-haq
Beersheba
(Bersabee)
Omer
Arad
Masada
El 'Arish
I S R A E L
Revivim
Sedom
Kefar Yeroham
Abu Aweigila
El 'Auja
Sede Boqer
'Ein Hatseva
Nevatim

DOCUMENTS

From sign to symbol,
From the mark to the line,
From the emblem to the metaphor,
The arcana of the inexpressible.

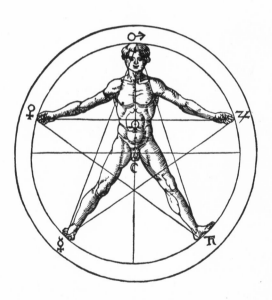

Sign theory

*The meanings of the word
sign are many and complex.
For linguists the sounds, or
phonemes, of a language and
the letters with which it is
written are signs. For artists
signs are emblems, symbols,
logos. Here is a sampling of
theoretical writings on this
fascinating concept.*

Previous page: a symbolic, Pythagorean
representation of man as a microcosmos,
from Heinrich Cornelius Agrippa (1486–1535),
De occulta philosophia, c. 1510.

Augustine

*Saint Augustine (AD 354–430), one of the
great philosophers of early Christianity,
was much concerned with rhetoric and
with the ways signs and symbols convey
meaning. Here are some excerpts from his
book on Christian learning.*

FROM BOOK I
All teaching is teaching of either things
or signs, but things are learnt through
signs. What I now call things in the
strict sense are things such as logs,
stones, sheep, and so on, which are not
employed to signify something....These
are things, but they are at the same time
signs of other things. There are other
signs whose whole function consists in
signifying. Words, for example: nobody
uses words except in order to signify
something. From this it may be understood what I mean by signs: those
things which are employed to signify
something. So every sign is also a thing,
since what is not a thing does not exist.
But it is not true that every thing is also
a sign. Therefore in my distinction of
things and signs, when I speak of
things, I shall speak of them in such a
way that even if some of them can be
employed to signify they do not impair
the arrangement by which I will treat
things first and signs later. And we
must be careful to remember that what
is under consideration at this stage is
the fact that things exist, not that they
signify something else besides
themselves....

FROM BOOK II
When I was writing about things I
began with the warning that attention
should be paid solely to the fact that
they existed, and not to anything
besides themselves that they might

Symbols from a variety of cultures, left to right: an ancient Greek *Triskelion,* emblem of victory; the Egyptian *Utchat,* the sacred Eye; a *Schemhamphora,* a medieval Kabbalistic magic circle, used for discovering buried treasure; a Roman *Cornucopia,* symbol of bounty; a Mameluk good-luck amulet.

signify. Now that I am discussing signs, I must say, conversely, that attention should not be paid to the fact that they exist, but rather to the fact that they are signs, or, in other words, that they signify. For a sign is a thing which of itself makes some other thing come to mind, besides the impression that it presents to the senses. So when we see a footprint we think that the animal whose footprint it is has passed by; when we see smoke we realize that there is fire beneath it; when we hear the voice of an animate being we observe its feeling; and when the trumpet sounds soldiers know they must advance or retreat or do whatever else the state of the battle demands.

Some signs are natural, others given. Natural signs are those which without a wish or any urge to signify cause something else besides themselves to be known from them, like smoke, which signifies fire....The expression of an angry or depressed person signifies an emotional state even if there is no such wish on the part of the person who is angry or depressed, and likewise any other emotion is revealed by the evidence of the face even if we are not seeking to reveal it....

Given signs are those which living things give to each other, in order to show, to the best of their ability, the emotions of their minds, or anything that they have felt or learnt. There is no reason for us to signify something (that is, to give a sign) except to express and transmit to another's mind what is in the mind of the person who gives the sign....Even the divinely given signs contained in the holy scriptures have been communicated to us by the human beings who wrote them....

Some of the signs by which people

Cruciform rock-art motifs from Corunna, Spain.

communicate their feelings to one another concern the eyes; most of them concern the ears, and a very small number concern the other senses. When we nod, we give a sign just to the eyes of the person whom we want, by means of that sign, to make aware of our wishes. Particular movements of the hands signify a great deal. By the movement of all their limbs, actors give certain signs to the cognoscenti and converse with the spectators' eyes, as it were; and it is through the eyes that flags and standards convey the wishes of military commanders. All these things are, to coin a phrase, visible words. But most signs, as I said, and especially verbal ones, concern the ears. A trumpet, a flute, and a lyre generally produce not just a pleasant sound but one that is also significant. But these signs are very few compared with words. Words have gained an altogether dominant role among humans in signifying the ideas conceived by the mind that a person wants to reveal....

But spoken words cease to exist as soon as they come into contact with the air, and their existence is no more lasting than that of their sound; hence the invention, in the form of letters, of signs of words....Even divine scripture, by which assistance is provided for the many serious disorders of the human will, after starting off in a single language, in which it could have been conveniently spread throughout the world, was circulated far and wide in the various language of translators....

But casual readers are misled by problems and ambiguities of many kinds, mistaking one thing for another. In some passages they find no meaning at all that they can grasp at, even falsely, so thick is the fog created by some obscure phrases. I have no doubt that this is all divinely predetermined, so that pride may be subdued by hard work and intellects which tend to despise things that are easily discovered may be rescued from boredom and reinvigorated....

There are two reasons why written texts fail to be understood: their meaning may be veiled either by unknown signs or by ambiguous signs. Signs are either literal or metaphorical. They are called literal when used to signify the things for which they were invented: as, for example, when we say *bovem* [ox], meaning the animal which we and all speakers of Latin call by that name. They are metaphorical when the actual things which we signify by the particular words are used to signify something else: when, for example, we say *bovem* and not only interpret these two syllables to mean the animal normally referred to by that name but also understand, by that animal, 'worker in the gospel', which is what scripture, as interpreted by the apostle Paul, means when it says, 'You shall not muzzle the ox that treads out the grain' [I Cor. 9:9 and I Tim. 5:18, quoting Deut. 25:4]....

As for metaphorical signs, any unfamiliar ones which puzzle the reader must be investigated partly through a

knowledge of languages, and partly through a knowledge of things....

All things which are meaningful to humans just because humans have decided that they should be so are human institutions. Some of them are superfluous and self-indulgent, others are useful and necessary. If the signs made by actors while dancing were naturally meaningful, rather than meaningful as a result of human insti-

The sun and moon in a Tatar drawing from Mongolia.

tution and agreement, an announcer would not have indicated to the Carthaginians, as each actor danced, what the dance meant, as he did in earlier days....Everyone aims at some degree of similarity when they use signs, making signs as similar as possible to the things which are signified. But because one thing can be similar to another in many ways, these signs are not generally understood unless accompanied by agreement. In the case of pictures and statues and other such representations, especially those made by experienced artists, nobody who sees the representation fails to recognize the things which they resemble. This whole category should be classed among superfluous human institutions, except when it makes a difference why or where or when or by whose authority one of them is made.

Saint Augustine,
On Christian Teaching, Books I, II,
AD C. 397

The science of language

The Swiss scholar Ferdinand de Saussure (1857–1913) revolutionized the methodical study of language, seeing it as a highly structured system of signs. His research provides the foundation of much modern linguistics and sign theory, which he named semiology.

PLACE OF LANGUAGE IN
HUMAN FACTS: SEMIOLOGY

Language is a social institution; but several features set it apart from other political, legal, etc. institutions. We must call in a new type of facts in order to illuminate the special nature of language.

Language is a system of signs that express ideas, and is therefore comparable to a system of writing, the alphabet of deaf-mutes, symbolic rites, polite formulas, military signals, etc. But it is the most important of all these systems.

A science that studies the life of signs within society is conceivable; it would be a part of social psychology and consequently of general psychology; I shall call it *semiology* (from Greek *sēmeîon* 'sign'). Semiology would show what constitutes signs, what laws govern them. Since the science does not yet exist, no one can say what it would be; but it has a right to existence, a place staked out in advance. Linguistics is

only a part of the general science of semiology; the laws discovered by semiology will be applicable to linguistics, and the latter will circumscribe a well-defined area within the mass of anthropological facts.

To determine the exact place of semiology is the task of the psychologist. The task of the linguist is to find out what makes language a special system within the mass of semiological data. This issue will be taken up again later; here I wish merely to call attention to one thing: if I have succeeded in assigning linguistics a place among the sciences, it is because I have related it to semiology.

Why has semiology not yet been recognized as an independent science with its own object like all the other sciences? Linguists have been going around in circles: language, better than anything else, offers a basis for understanding the semiological problem; but language must, to put it correctly, be studied in itself; heretofore language has almost always been studied in connection with something else, from other viewpoints.

There is first of all the superficial notion of the general public: people see nothing more than a name-giving system in language, thereby prohibiting any research into its true nature.

Then there is the viewpoint of the psychologist, who studies the sign-mechanism in the individual; this is the easiest method, but it does not lead beyond individual execution and does not reach the sign, which is social.

Or even when signs are studied from a social viewpoint, only the traits that attach language to the other social institutions—those that are more or less voluntary—are emphasized; as a

Albrecht Dürer's Renaissance engraving *Melencholia I* is packed with intricate iconographical details: the winged figure is a personification of Melancholy, who sits lost in gloomy thought. The compasses in her hand and the tools of architecture, drafting, and sculpture strewn on the ground symbolize art. A scale and an hourglass indicate the passage of time. A mathematical magic square, a sphere, and a polyhedron represent science and geometry—the measurement of space. The title banner is carried by a bat, symbol of the devil and of melancholy, sweeping us into the sunset.

result, the goal is by-passed and the specific characteristics of semiological systems in general and of language in particular are completely ignored.

For the distinguishing characteristic of the sign—but the one that is least apparent at first sight—is that in some way it always eludes the individual or social will.

In short, the characteristic that distinguishes semiological systems from all other institutions shows up clearly only in language where it manifests itself in the things which are studied least, and the necessity or specific value of a semiological science is therefore not clearly recognized. But to me the language problem is mainly semio-logical, and all developments derive their significance from that important fact. If we are to discover the true nature of language we must learn what it has in common with all other semiological systems; linguistic forces that seem very important at first glance (e.g., the role of the vocal apparatus) will receive only secondary consideration if they serve only to set language apart from the other systems. This procedure will do more than to clarify the linguistic problem. By studying rites, customs, etc. as signs, I believe that we shall throw new light on the facts and point up the need for including them in a science of semiology and explaining them by its laws.

Ferdinand de Saussure,
Course in General Linguistics, 1916,
translated by Wade Baskin, 1959

Art as a network of signs

In 1939 the German-born art historian Erwin Panofsky (1892–1968) published Studies in Iconology, *in which he explored the ways that a work of art incorporates, uses, and invents visual signs and sign systems.*

ICONOGRAPHY AND ICONOLOGY
Iconography is that branch of the history of art which concerns itself with the subject matter or meaning of works of art, as opposed to their form. Let us, then, try to define the distinction between subject matter or meaning on the one hand, and form on the other.

When an acquaintance greets me on the street by lifting his hat, what I see from a formal point of view is nothing but the change of certain details within a configuration forming part of the general pattern of color, lines and volumes which constitutes my world of vision. When I identify, as I automatically do, this configuration as an object (gentleman), and the change of detail as an event (hat-lifting), I have already overstepped the limits of purely formal perception and entered a first sphere of subject matter or meaning. The meaning thus perceived is of an elementary and easily understandable nature, and we shall call it the factual meaning; it is apprehended by simply identifying certain visible forms with certain objects known to me from practical experience, and by identifying the change in their relations with certain actions or events.

Now the objects and events thus identified will naturally produce a certain reaction within myself. From the way my acquaintance performs his action I may be able to sense whether he is in a good or bad humor, and whether his feelings towards me are indifferent, friendly or hostile. These psychological nuances will invest the gestures of my acquaintance with a further meaning which we shall call expressional. It differs from the factual one in that it is apprehended, not by simple identification, but by "empathy." To understand it, I need a certain sensitivity, but this sensitivity is still part of my practical experience, that is, of my everyday familiarity with objects and events. Therefore both the factual and the expressional meaning may be classified together: they constitute the class of primary or natural meanings.

However, my realization that the lifting of the hat stands for a greeting belongs in an altogether different realm of interpretation. This form of salute is peculiar to the Western world and is a residue of mediaeval chivalry: armed men used to remove their helmets to make clear their peaceful intentions and their confidence in the peaceful intentions of others. Neither an Australian bushman nor an ancient Greek could be expected to realize that the lifting of a hat is not only a practical event with certain expressional connotations, but also a sign of politeness. To understand this significance of the gentleman's action I must not only be familiar with the practical world of objects and events, but also with the more-than-practical world of customs and cultural traditions peculiar to a certain civilization. Conversely, my acquaintance could not feel impelled to greet me by lifting his hat were he not conscious of the significance of this act. As for the expressional connotations which accompany his action, he may or may not be conscious of them. Therefore, when I interpret the lifting of a hat as a polite greeting, I recognize in it a meaning which may be called secondary or conventional; it differs from the primary or natural one in that it is intelligible instead of being sensible, and in that it has been consciously imparted to the practical action by which it is conveyed.

And finally: besides constituting a natural event in space and time, besides naturally indicating moods or feelings, besides conveying a conventional greeting, the action of my acquaintance can reveal to an experienced observer all that goes to make up his "personality." This personality is conditioned by his being a man of the twentieth century, by his national, social and educational background, by the previous history of his life and by his present surroundings; but it is also distinguished by an individual manner of viewing things and reacting to the world which, if rationalized, would have to be called a philosophy. In the isolated action of a polite greeting all these factors do not manifest themselves comprehensively, but nevertheless symptomatically. We could not construct a mental portrait of the man on the basis of this single action, but only by co-ordinating a large number of similar observations and by interpreting them in connection with our general information as to his period, nationality, class, intellectual traditions and so forth. Yet all the qualities which this mental portrait would show explicitly are implicitly inherent in every single action; so that, conversely, every single action can be interpreted in the light of those qualities.

The meaning thus discovered may be called the intrinsic meaning or content; it is essential where the two other kinds of meaning, the primary or natural and the secondary or conventional, are phenomenal. It may be defined as a unifying principle which underlies and explains both the visible event and its intelligible significance, and which determines even the form in which the visible event takes shape. This intrinsic meaning or content is, normally, as much above the sphere of conscious volition as the expressional meaning is beneath this sphere.

Transferring the results of this analysis from everyday life to a work of art, we can distinguish in its subject matter or meaning the same three strata:

1. *Primary or natural subject matter,* subdivided into *factual* and *expressional.* It is apprehended by identifying pure forms, that is: certain configurations of line and color, or certain peculiarly shaped lumps of

The Virgin Mary and Saint John, detail of Matthias Grünewald, the *Isenheim Altarpiece,* 1510–15.

bronze or stone, as representations of natural objects such as human beings, animals, plants, houses, tools and so forth; by identifying their mutual relations as events; and by perceiving such expressional qualities as the mournful character of a pose or gesture, or the homelike and peaceful atmosphere of an interior. The world of pure forms thus recognized as carriers of primary or natural meanings may be called the world of artistic motifs. An enumeration of these motifs would be a pre-iconographical description of the work of art.

2. *Secondary or conventional subject matter.* It is apprehended by realizing that a male figure with a knife represents St. Bartholomew, that a female figure with a peach in her hand is a personification of veracity, that a group of figures seated at a dinner table in a certain arrangement and in certain poses represents the Last Supper, or that two figures fighting each other in a certain manner represent the Combat of Vice and Virtue. In doing this we connect artistic motifs and combinations of artistic motifs (compositions) with themes or concepts. Motifs thus recognized as carriers of a secondary or conventional meaning may be called images, and combinations of images are what the ancient theorists of art called *invenzioni;* we are wont to call them stories and allegories. The identification of such images, stories and allegories is the domain of what is normally referred to as "iconography."…

3. *Intrinsic meaning or content.* It is apprehended by ascertaining those underlying principles which reveal the basic attitude of a nation, a period, a class, a religious or philosophical persuasion—qualified by one person-

ality and condensed into one work. Needless to say, these principles are manifested by, and therefore throw light on, both "compositional methods" and "iconographical significance." In the fourteenth and fifteenth centuries, for instance (the earliest examples can be dated around 1300), the traditional type of the Nativity with the Virgin Mary reclining in bed or on a couch was frequently replaced by a new one which shows the Virgin kneeling before the Child in adoration. From a compositional point of view this change means, roughly speaking, the substitution of a triangular scheme for a rectangular one; from an iconographical point of view, it means the introduction of a new theme to be formulated in writing by such authors as Pseudo-Bonaventure and St. Bridget. But at the same time it reveals a new emotional attitude peculiar to the later phases of the Middle Ages. A really exhaustive interpretation of the intrinsic meaning or content might even show that the technical procedures characteristic of a certain country, period, or artist, for instance Michelangelo's preference for sculpture in stone instead of in bronze, or the peculiar use of hatchings in his drawings, are symptomatic of the same basic attitude that is discernible in all the other specific qualities of his style. In thus conceiving of pure forms, motifs, images, stories and allegories as manifestations of underlying principles, we interpret all these elements as what Ernst Cassirer has called "symbolical" values.... The discovery and interpretation of these "symbolical" values (which are often unknown to the artist himself and may even emphatically differ from what he consciously intended to express) is the object of what we may call "iconology" as opposed to "iconography."

The suffix "graphy" derives from the Greek verb *graphein*, "to write"; it implies a purely descriptive, often even statistical, method of procedure. Iconography is, therefore, a description and classification of images much as ethnography is a description and classification of human races: it is a limited and, as it were, ancillary study which informs us as to when and where specific themes were visualized by which specific motifs.... [Iconography] collects and classifies the evidence but does not consider itself obliged or entitled to investigate the genesis and significance of this evidence: the interplay between the various "types"; the influence of theological, philosophical or political ideas; the purposes and inclinations of individual artists and patrons; the correlation between intelligible concepts and the visible form which they assume in each specific case. In short, iconography considers only a part of all those elements which enter into the intrinsic content of a work of art and must be made explicit if the perception of this content is to become articulate and communicable....

Iconology...is a method of interpretation which arises from synthesis rather than analysis. And as the correct identification of motifs is the prerequisite of their correct iconographical analysis, so is the correct analysis of images, stories and allegories the prerequisite of their correct iconological interpretation.

Erwin Panofsky,
Studies in Iconology,
1939

The Italian semiologist Umberto Eco (b. 1932) has long been interested in the way signs work: how a word comes to represent a thing, and how its meanings may be altered or revised. In addition to writing many scholarly books on semiotics and language, with a focus on the mechanics of metaphor, he has pursued these issues in several novels. In a medieval murder mystery two 14th-century monks discuss whether a unicorn may be considered real because it has been described in books.

"But is the unicorn a falsehood? It's the sweetest of animals and a noble symbol. It stands for Christ, and for chastity...."

"So it is said, Adso. But many tend to believe that it's a fable, an invention of the pagans."...

"But what use is the unicorn to you if your intellect doesn't believe in it?"

"...The unicorn of the books is like a [hoof] print. If the print exists, there must have existed some thing whose print it is."

"But different from the print, you say."

"Of course. The print does not always have the same shape as the body that impressed it, and it doesn't always derive from the pressure of a body. At times it reproduces the impression a body has left in our mind: it is the print of an idea. The idea is sign of things, and the image is sign of the idea, sign of a sign. But from the image I reconstruct, if not the body, the idea that others had of it."

"And this is enough for you?"

"No, because true learning must not be content with ideas, which are, in fact, signs, but must discover things in their individual truth."

Umberto Eco,
The Name of the Rose, 1980,
translated by William Weaver

The semantics of metaphor

If all codes were as simple and univocal as Morse code, there would be no problem. It is true that a great deal which the code cannot anticipate can be said with Morse code; it is equally true that one can transmit in Morse code instructions capable of modifying the code itself. This can occur because Morse code's signifiers take, as the signified, alphabetical signifiers which in turn refer us to that complex system of systems known as language—by language meaning, in this case, the total competence of a speaking subject and thus the system of semantic systems as well, that is, the total form of the content. Yet it is precisely this sort of competence, not entirely analyzable, which we have decided to call "code" as well, not for the sake of simple analogy but in order to broaden the scope of the term.

How can it be, then, that this code, which in principle ought to have structured the speaking subject's entire cultural system, is able to generate both factual messages which refer to original experiences and, above all, messages which place in doubt the very structure of the code itself?

The fact that the code, in referring to predictable cultural entities, nonetheless allows us to assign new semiotic marks to them, is singular to that feature of the code called "rule-governed creativity." That the code allows for factual judgments poses no difficulties either; the very nature of the code, which is arbitrary, explains how it can, by manipulating signifiers, refer to new signifieds produced in response to new experiences. It also explains why, once issued, factual judgments can be integrated into the

Detail of an allegory of *Vanity*, or *Sight*, a 15th-century Netherlandish tapestry from the series *The Lady with the Unicorn*. In medieval courtly art and literature the tale of the maiden and the unicorn is often symbolic of love. The unicorn may also represent Christ.

code in such a way as to create new possibilities for semiotic judgment. How, though, does this "rule-changing creativity" work?

Even prior to the specifically aesthetic usage of language, the first example of such creativity is provided in common speech by the use of different types of metaphors and thus of rhetorical figures. A series of problems that touch on rhetorical devices will allow us to respond to these questions. In the case under consideration we will at present deal with the problem of interaction between metaphoric mechanisms and metonymic mechanisms; to these one can probably ascribe the entire range of tropes, figures of speech, and figures of thought....

Each metaphor can be traced back to a subjacent chain of metonymic

Icons and spot illustrations used in newspaper editorials.

connections which constitute the framework of the code and upon which is based the constitution of any semantic field, whether partial or (in theory) global....

Any explanation which restores language to metaphor or which shows that, in the domain of language, it is possible to invent metaphors returns to an analogical (and hence metaphorical) explanation of language and presumes an idealist doctrine of linguistic creativity. If, on the other hand, the explanation of the creativity of language (presupposed by the existence of metaphors) is based on metonymic chains based in turn on identifiable semantic structures, it is then possible to bring the problem of creativity back to a description of language which depends upon a model susceptible to translation in binary terms. In other words, it is possible (even though for experimental purposes and only for limited parts of the Global Semantic System) to construct an automaton capable of generating and understanding metaphors....

The majority of our messages, in everyday life or in academic philosophy, are lined with metaphors. The problem of the creativity of language emerges, not only in the privileged domain of poetic discourse, but each time that language—in order to designate something that culture has not yet assimilated (and this 'something' may be external or internal to the circle of semiosis)—must *invent* combinatory possibilities or semantic couplings not anticipated by the code.

Metaphor, in this sense, appears as a new semantic coupling not preceded by any stipulation of the code (but which generates a new stipulation of the code). In this sense, as we shall see, it assumes a value in regard to communication and, indirectly, to knowledge.

Umberto Eco,
The Role of the Reader: Explorations in the Semiotics of Texts, 1979,
translated by William Weaver, 1983

Interrupted meanings

Roland Barthes (1915–80), the influential French critic, studied sign theory and wrote in an elliptical, poetic style that explored the ways meaning may be transformed or interrupted by language itself. He was fascinated by the way dissimilar cultures use signs; here he looks at differences between Europe and Japan.

In this 1849 print a Japanese actor of the traditional Kabuki theater displays its stylized gestures.

Why, in the West, is politeness regarded with suspicion? Why does courtesy pass for a distance (if not an evasion, in fact) or a hypocrisy? Why is an "informal" relation (as we so greedily say) more desirable than a coded one?

Occidental impoliteness is based on a certain mythology of the "person." Topologically, Western man is reputed to be double, composed of a social, factitious, false "outside" and of a personal, authentic "inside" (the site of divine communication). According to this schema, the human "person" is that site filled by nature (or by divinity, or by guilt), girdled, closed by a social envelope which is anything but highly regarded: the polite gesture (when it is postulated) is the sign of respect exchanged from one plenitude to the other, across the worldly limit (i.e., in spite and by the intermediary of this limit). However, as soon as the "inside" of the person is judged respectable, it is logical to recognize this person more suitably by denying all interest to his worldly envelope: hence it is the supposedly frank, brutal, naked relation, stripped (it is thought) of all signaletics, indifferent to any intermediary code, which will best respect the other's individual value: to be impolite is to be true—so speaks (logically enough) our Western morality. For if there is indeed a human "person" (dense, emphatic, centered, sacred), it is doubtless this person which in an initial movement we claim to "salute" (with the head, the lips, the body); but my own person, inevitably entering into conflict with the other's plenitude, can gain recognition only by rejecting all mediation of the factitious and by affirming the integrity (highly ambiguous, this word: physical and moral) of its "inside"; and in a second impulse, I shall reduce my salute, I shall pretend to make it natural, spontaneous, disencumbered, purified of any code: I shall be scarcely affable, or affable according to an apparently invented fantasy, like the Princess of Parma (in Proust) signaling the breadth of her income and the height of her rank (i.e., her way of being "full" of things and of constituting herself a person), not by a distant stiffness of manner, but by the willed "simplicity" of her manners: how simple I am, how affable I am, how frank I am, how much I am *someone* is what Occidental impoliteness says.

The other politeness, by the scrupulosity of its codes, the distinct graphism of its gestures, and even when it seems to us exaggeratedly respectful (i.e., to our eyes, "humiliating") because we read it, in our manner, according to a metaphysics of the person—this politeness is a certain exercise of the void (as we might expect within a strong code but one signifying "nothing"). Two bodies bow very low before one another (arms, knees, head always remaining in a decreed place), according to subtly coded degrees of depth. Or again (on an old image): in order to give a present, I bow down, virtually to the level of the floor, and to answer me, my partner does the same: one and the same low line, that of the ground, joins the giver, the recipient, and the stake of the protocol, a box which may well contain nothing— or virtually nothing; a graphic form (inscribed in the space of the room) is thereby given to the act of exchange, in which, by this form, is erased any greediness (the gift remains suspended between two disappearances). The salutation here can be withdrawn from any humiliation or any vanity, because it literally salutes *no one;* it is not the sign of a communication— closely watched, condescending and precautionary—between two autarchies, two personal empires (each ruling over its Ego, the little realm of which it holds the "key"); it is only the

feature of a network of forms in which nothing is halted, knotted, profound. *Who is saluting whom?* Only such a question justifies the salutation, inclines it to the bow, the obeisance, and glorifies thereby not meaning but the inscription of meaning, and gives to a posture which we read as excessive the very reserve of a gesture from which any signified is inconceivably absent. *The Form is Empty,* says—and repeats —a Buddhist aphorism. This is what is expressed, through a practice of forms (a word whose plastic meaning and worldly meaning are here indissociable), by the politeness of the salutation, the bowing of two bodies which inscribe but do not prostrate themselves. Our ways of speaking are very vicious, for if I say that in that country politeness is a religion, I let it be understood that there is something sacred in it; the expression should be canted so as to suggest that religion there is merely a politeness, or better still, that religion has been replaced by politeness.

Roland Barthes,
Empire of Signs, 1970,
translated by Richard Howard, 1982

Thought in motion

Another French philosopher, Henri Bergson (1859–1941) was interested in both the technical aspects of signs and the human values and problems of communication.

To hear some theorists discourse on sensory aphasia, we might imagine that they had never considered with any care the structure of a sentence. They argue as if a sentence were composed of nouns which call up the images of things. What becomes of those parts of speech, of which the precise function is to establish, between images, relations and shades of meaning of every kind? Is it said that each of such words still expresses and evokes a material image, more confused, no doubt, but yet determined? Consider then the host of different relations which can be expressed by the same word, according to the place it occupies and the terms which it unites. Is it urged that these are the refinements of a highly-developed language, but that speech is possible with concrete nouns that all summon up images of things? No doubt it is, but the more primitive the language you speak with me and the poorer in words which express relations, the more you are bound to allow for my mind's activity, since you compel me to find out the relations which you leave unexpressed: which amounts to saying that you abandon more and more the hypothesis that each verbal image goes up and fetches down its corresponding idea. In truth, there is here only a question of degree: every language, whether elaborated or crude, leaves many more things to be understood than it is able to express. Essentially discontinuous, since it proceeds by juxtaposing words, speech can only indicate by a few guide-posts placed here and there the chief stages in the movement of thought. That is why I can indeed understand your speech if I start from a thought analogous to your own, and follow its windings by the aid of verbal images which are so many sign-posts that show me the way from time to time. But I shall never be able to understand it if I start from the verbal images themselves, because between two consecutive verbal images there is a gulf which no amount of concrete representations can ever fill. For images can never be anything but things, and thought is a movement.

Henri Bergson,
Matter and Memory, 1896,
translated by Nancy M. Paul and
W. Scott Palmer, 1959

Ritual colors

Symbols are not always objects, emblems, or logos. A phrase of music may be symbolic—think of the triumphant notes of a trumpet signaling victory, or the long, slow minor tones of a funeral dirge. Perhaps the most widespread abstract symbols are colors, which convey so much information so efficiently. In a classic anthropological study of African rituals, a scholar explores the meanings of three especially important symbolic colors: red, white, and black.

THE SIGNIFICANCE OF THE BASIC COLOR TRIAD

In ethnographic literature, it is noteworthy that among societies that make ritual use of all three colors [red, black, and white], the critical situation in which these appear together is initiation. Each may appear separately as a sign of the general character of a rite; thus red may be a persistent motif in hunting rites among the Ndembu and white in rites dealing with lactation or village ancestral shades. At the initiation of juniors into the rights and duties and values of seniors, all three colors receive equal emphasis. In my view this is because they epitomize the main kinds of universal human organic experience. In many societies these colors have explicit reference to certain fluids, secretions or waste products of the human body. Red is universally a symbol of blood, white is frequently a symbol of breast milk and semen.... Each of the colors in all societies is multivocal, having a wide fan of connotations, but nevertheless the human physiological component is seldom absent wherever reliable native exegesis is available. Initiation rites often draw their symbolism from the situation of parturition and first lactation, where, in nature, blood, water, feces, and milk are present.

I am going to throw caution to the winds for the sake of stimulating controversy and state boldly that:

1. Among the earliest symbols produced by man are the three colors representing products of the human body whose emission, spilling, or production is associated with a heightening of emotion. In other words, culture, the superorganic, has an intimate connection with the organic in its early stages, with the awareness of powerful physical experiences.

2. These heightened bodily experiences are felt to be informed with a power in excess of that normally possessed by the individual; its source may be located in the cosmos or in society; analogues of physical experience may then be found wherever the same colors occur in nature; or else experience of social relations in heightened emotional circumstances may be classified under a color rubric.

3. The colors represent heightened physical experience transcending the experiencer's normal condition; they are therefore conceived as deities...or mystical powers, as the sacred over against the profane.

4. The physical experiences associated with the three colors are also experiences of social relationships: white = semen is linked to mating between man and woman; white = milk is linked to the mother-child tie; red = maternal blood is linked to the mother-child tie and also the processes of group recruitment and social placement; red = bloodshed is connected with war, feud, conflict, social discontinuities; red = obtaining and preparation of animal food = status of hunter or herder, male productive role in the sexual division of labor, etc.; red = transmission of blood from generation to generation = an index of membership in a corporate group; black = excreta or bodily dissolution = transition from one social status to another viewed as mystical death; black = rain clouds or fertile earth = unity of widest recognized group sharing same life values.

5. While it is possible to find many references to body fluids in white and red symbolism, few societies specifically connect black with processes and products of catabolism and decay, for example, with decayed or clotted blood. It is possible that black which, as we have seen, often means "death," a "fainting fit," "sleep," or "darkness" primarily represents falling into unconsciousness, the experience of a "black-out." Among Ndembu, and in many other societies, both white and red may stand for life. When they are paired in ritual, white may stand for one alleged polarity of life, such as masculinity or vegetable food, while red may represent its opposite, such as femininity or meat. On the other hand, white may represent "peace" and red "war"; both are conscious activities as distinct from black which stands for inactivity and the cessation of consciousness.

6. Not only do the three colors stand for basic human experiences of the

body (associated with the gratification of libido, hunger, aggressive and excretory drives, and with fear, anxiety, and submissiveness), they also provide a kind of primordial classification of reality.... The color triad white-red-black represents the archetypal man as a pleasure-pain process. The perception of these colors and of triadic and dyadic relations in the cosmos and in society, either directly or metaphorically, is a derivative of primordial psychobiological experience—experience that can be fully attained only in human mutuality. It needs two to copulate, two to suckle and wean, two to fight and kill, and three to form a family. The multitude of interlaced classifications that make up ideological systems controlling social relationships are derivatives, divested of affectual accompaniments, of these primordial twos and threes. The basic three are sacred because they have the power "to carry the man away," to overthrow his normal powers of resistance. Though immanent in his body, they appear to transcend his consciousness. By representing these "forces" or "strands of life" by color symbols in a ritual context, men may have felt that they could domesticate or control these forces for social ends, but the forces and the symbols for them are biologically, psychologically, and logically prior to social classifications by moieties, clans, sex totems, and all the rest. Since the experiences the three colors represent are common to all mankind, we do not have to invoke diffusion to explain their wide distribution. We do have to invoke diffusion to explain why other colors, such as yellow, saffron, gold, blue, green, purple, etc., are ritually important in certain cultures. We must also look to processes of culture contact to explain differences in the senses attributed to the basic colors in different regions. The point I am trying to make here is that the three colors white-red-black for the simpler societies are not merely differences in the visual perception of parts of the spectrum: they are abridgments or condensations of whole realms of psychobiological experience involving reason and all the senses and concerned with primary group relationships. It is only by subsequent abstraction from these configurations that the other modes of social classification employed by mankind arose.

Victor Turner,
*The Forest of Symbols:
Aspects of Ndembu Ritual,*
1967

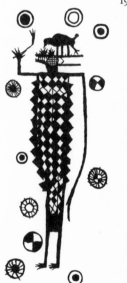

A Senufo painted-cloth image representing a fire-spitter masquerader, from Côte d'Ivoire, West Africa.

Signs and the origins of writing

Among the earliest images in prehistoric art are abstract sequences of marks, dots, and patterns. These are definitely signs, but what are their meanings? Are they the earliest forms of writing?

A prehistoric rock engraving from Catalonia in eastern Spain, possibly a human figure carrying a child.

Signs at the beginning of human history

The eminent prehistorian André Leroi-Gourhan was one of the first modern scholars to examine the abstract signs and marks in Paleolithic caves.

It was their widespread occurrence in cave art that focused attention on the [abstract] signs at the beginning of the twentieth century. The Abbé Breuil published drawings of a large number of them. Study of the El Castillo and La Pasiega caves…first aroused his interest —and consequently that of other prehistorians—in the strange configurations which are found by the dozen in these two Spanish caves, in out-of-the-way corners and in the midst of the main panels…upstrokes and downstrokes, horizontal lines, and rectangles, the latter often compartmented like heraldic coats-of-arms.…Because certain of these signs are sometimes found on a bison, a mammoth, or the head of a hind, other prehistorians supposed that they must represent animal snares.…

The real importance of the signs only emerged later, after an explanatory series of statistical tests. Statistically, they proved to belong to two sets: one of single dots, rows of dots, short strokes, and barbed signs; the other of ovals, triangles, rectangles, and brace-shaped signs. Since one set occurs at the entrances and in the back-cave areas, and the other in the central portions, it became obvious that the two series correspond to the same system of distribution as the animal figures.…An important number of signs of the first set (located at the entrances and the backs of the caves) turn up in the central groups [of animal paintings]. The rule of complementarity, according to which

Paleolithic signs in the Lascaux cave divided into categories by Leroi-Gourhan.

horses accompany bison in the central panels, thus applies also to these signs.... Generally speaking, every sign from the "enclosed" set on the central panels is matched by a sign of the "dot and stroke" set. And the converse was also entirely true: the signs from the "enclosed" set are just as rare at the entrances and in the back-cave areas as are bison and oxen....

I found myself in the end confronted with a system of unexpected complexity —the skeleton of a religious thought, as impervious to my understanding, moreover, as a comparative study of the iconography of sixty cathedrals would be to an archaeologist from Mars.

André Leroi-Gourhan,
Treasures of Prehistoric Art, 1967,
translated by Norbert Guterman

Nonfigurative signs

Paul Bahn expanded upon the research of Leroi-Gourhan.

The non-figurative category of Palaeolithic markings was neglected until relatively recently, for the simple reason that it seemed uninteresting, or impossible to explain or define. Many lines, as mentioned earlier, were simply ignored as *'traits parasites'*. Nowadays, however, thanks to the attention paid to the abstract 'signs' by Leroi-Gourhan and to the discovery of similar non-figurative motifs in Australia and elsewhere we have to come to terms with the possibility that these marks may have been of equal, if not greater, importance to Palaeolithic people than the 'recognisable' figures to which we have devoted so much attention. Certainly, it has been estimated that non-figurative marks are two or three times more abundant than figurative, and in some areas far more: for example, on 1,200 engraved pieces of bone and antler from 26 Magdalenian sites in Cantabria, there are only 70 identifiable animals—all other motifs seem non-figurative....

A prehistoric rock painting from the Catalan Pyrenees, Spain.

[This category] comprises a tremendously wide range of motifs, from a single dot or line to complex constructions, and to extensive panels of apparently unstructured linear marks. There are significant differences in content between portable and parietal examples, which make it extremely difficult to date parietal 'signs', particularly in cases where they constitute the only decoration and figurative images are absent, as at Santián and other sites. Even in caves with both figurative and non-figurative images on the walls, 'signs' can be either totally isolated, clustered on their own panels or in their own chambers, or closely associated with the figurative—and sometimes all of these.

In the past, certain shapes were assumed to be narrative or picto-graphic: i.e. to represent schematised objects on the basis of ethnographic comparisons or, more often, subjective assessment of what they 'looked like': hence, we have terms such as 'tectiforms' (huts), 'claviforms' (clubs), 'scutiforms' (shields), 'aviforms' (birds), 'penniforms' (feathers), etc. These are no longer taken literally but, as they have entered the literature so decisively, are retained simply as rough guides to particular shapes. Even if these motifs were ultimately derived from real objects, they could now be purely abstract, although it is impossible for us to separate them fully from 'realistic' figures: some signs may indeed be schematised or abbreviated (or unfinished!) versions of some object. Some authors now regard 'signs' as 'ideomorphs'—i.e. representations of ideas rather than objects, but we simply don't know whether they are real or abstract or both.

We inevitably apply our understand-ing to what we see; our background, culture and art history come into play, and hence the early scholars tried to translate some signs as if they were hieroglyphics, in the vain hope of finding a Palaeolithic Rosetta Stone.

Even if these signs *were* representational, their meaning would be far from straightforward without an informant: for example, among the Walbiri of Australia, a simple circle can mean a hill, tree, campsite, circular path, egg, breast, nipple, entrance into or exit from the ground and a host of other things; similarly, 'translation' of simple signs and pictographs in North America can often produce differing and unexpected results. A mere resemblance of shape does not necessarily mean that a motif is an image of an object.

What is clear is that the simpler motifs are more abundant and widespread, as one would expect, since they could have been invented in many places and periods independently. The more complex forms, however, show extraordinary variability and are more restricted in space and time, to the extent that they have been seen as 'ethnic markers', perhaps delineating Palaeolithic groups of some sort: hence, 'quadrilateral' signs seem concentrated in Dordogne, particularly at Lascaux and Gabillou; a different kind of 'quadrilateral' is found in a Cantabrian group of caves (Castillo, La Pasiega and Las Chimeneas, all in the same hill, together with Altamira, some 20 km [c. 12 miles] away); 'tectiforms' are found in the Les Eyzies region (Dordogne), in a small group of caves only a few kilometres apart, including Font de Gaume and Bernifal; very similar 'aviforms' are known at Cougnac and Pech-Merle, 35 km [c. 21 miles] apart; triangles are predominantly found in the centre of Spain, but are rare in Cantabria; perhaps most remarkable of all is the distribution of true 'clavi-forms', which are known in Ariège (Niaux, Trois Frères, Tuc d'Audoubert,

	MONT BEGO	ARIÈGE
Signe en flèche		
Arboriforme		
Demi-arboriforme		
Arciforme		
Arbalétiforme		
Signe en phi		
Pectiniforme		
Scalariforme		

Categories of prehistoric signs found in the Mont Bégo area of the Alps and in the Ariège region of France.

Le Portel, Fontanet, Mas d'Azil) and in Cantabria (Pindal, La Cullalvera) some 500 km [c. 300 miles] away (and perhaps also at Lascaux)....

Leroi-Gourhan divided 'signs' into two basic groups, the 'thin' and the 'full', which he linked to a sexual symbolism (phallic and vulvar); he later added a third group, that of the dots. In view of the wide range of shapes on display, such a division was far too simplistic and schematic; using geometric criteria, other scholars have proposed seven or even a dozen classes of parietal sign but still found some very hard to fit in.

A Bronze Age rock pictograph, possibly of a man with raised arms facing a pack of dogs, in the Val Camonica in northern Italy.

Similarly, the non-figurative motifs in portable art have been receiving an increasing amount of attention lately, and likewise have been divided into different groups. Meg Conkey, for example, has sought out the basic units of decorative systems in Cantabrian portable art, and their structural interrelations. In a sample of 1,200 pieces, she found a set of about 200 distinct 'design elements', which she organised into 57 'classes'. Her analysis revealed that a core set of 15 elements was used throughout the Magdalenian, and was widespread within and outside the region. As with the parietal signs, therefore, it will be necessary to focus on the more complex designs in order to identify regional variations in style (and possibly distinct social groups of some kind).

In both parietal and portable art, a full survey of the presence and interrelationships of different motifs, as well as of their association with each other and with other figures, is required, but will entail a more complete published corpus than we have, followed by computer analysis. It is the presence and absence of particular combinations which is revealing: in parietal signs, for example, very few binary combinations occur out of the range of possibilities, and only signs found in binary combinations also occur in 'triads'. Clearly these marks were not set down at random, but follow some set of rules and simple laws.

Can they therefore be seen as a primitive form of writing? Theories about this go back to the discovery of portable art, when a variety of enigmatic motifs associated with animal figures were seen as possible artists' signatures by a number of scholars including Lartet, Garrigou and Piette. It is inevitable that, despite their wide variety of shapes, some of the Palaeolithic signs will resemble some of the simpler characters in certain early forms of writing; after all, the range of possible basic marks is somewhat limited. It has recently been claimed that some Palaeolithic signs have very close analogies with characters and letters in ancient written languages in the Mediterranean, the Indus valley and China, but, as with resemblances to objects, this does not necessarily prove anything. As far as parietal signs are concerned, it often appears to be their presence which was important, rather than their layout or orientation; instead of forming a script, they were sometimes joined through superposition, juxtaposition or actual integration to form composites.

Where motifs on portable objects are concerned, however, it is still possible that they include some sort of 'pre-writing'; we simply don't know. What is almost certain is that the meaning of the signs and marks, no matter how abstract they may appear to us, must have been clear to the maker and to those who saw and/or used them. We can see this today with our road signs and warnings: some have meanings obvious to everyone, others have to be learnt, but all are known to those who operate within that system.

Paul Bahn and Jean Vertut,
Images of the Ice Age, 1988

Theories and myths of the origins of writing

When, where, and how did writing first begin? For millennia myths and tales have offered answers to this intriguing question.

EARLY MESOPOTAMIAN AND EGYPTIAN MYTHS

Twentieth-century accounts of the origins of writing differ substantially from the earliest myths, which generally credit the gift of writing to divinity. In a multivolume study of the diversity of languages in early cultures, Arno Borst found such accounts common to all cultures in the process of completing the transition from oral tradition to historical consciousness. As in the Tower of Babel myth, they are the product of a universal belief in religion as the justification for existence. It was, therefore, natural to seek a relationship between language and religion, to believe that language was a gift of God to man and that God granted the gift of writing to bridge man's growing separation from his origins. One should not reject early myths out of hand as irrational effusions of unscientific minds. In many cases, early myths contain concepts which today have become essential to our views of the past; in others, they reveal historical perceptions that can aid our comprehension of the early stages of writing.

Pictorial Origin of Ten Cuneiform Signs

Bird
Fish
Donkey
Ox
Sun
Grain
Orchard
Plough
Boomerang
Foot

The development of Mesopotamian cuneiform script, illustrated with ten examples.

Unfortunately for posterity, Sumerian mythographers did not devise a systematic formulation of their cosmological beliefs, and information about the origins of their writing must be gleaned from their myths piece by piece. Political and social changes, historical and regional shifts in the pantheon of divine beings occlude even more the cosmology of the land that came to be known first as Sumer, later as Sumer and

Akkad, and still later as Babylonia. This in part helps clarify why the creation of language and writing was attributed in varying degrees to Nabû, Tashmetum (Nabû's consort), Nidaba ("great scribe of heaven"), and Enlil. There is, however, consistent evidence that Sumerian theologians, like those in Egypt and Canaan, believed in the creative power of the divine word ("Your [Enlil's] word— it is plants, your word—it is grain, / Your word is the floodwater, the life of all the lands") and that most Sumerian scribes attributed that power to their patron Nabû (the biblical Nebo [Isa. 46.1]). Nabû, foremost son of the highest deity of the pantheon, after whom kings such as Nebuchadnezzar (562 BC, 2 Kings 24.1) were named, was revered as "the inventor of the writing of scribes," "the unrivaled scribe," "the scribe of the gods, wielder of the reed-pen."

As in Sumer, the birth of writing in Egypt was associated with several deities, including a goddess of writing (Seshat) and even a deity of perverse speech. Most Egyptian documents name Thoth as the creator of writing. Thoth, or Tehuti, has been linked through his Egyptian name "Dhwt(y)" ("messenger" or "measurer") and one of his many mythical functions as son and representative of the sun god, Re, to the Greek messenger of the gods, Hermes, and his Roman counterpart, Mercury.

Extant Egyptian texts portray Thoth as the supreme intelligence, who during the Creation uttered words which were magically transformed into objects of the material world. As was suggested in the examples from Mesopotamian mythology, these utterances also contain no clear differentiation between language and writing. Borst argues that the failure to distinguish between the

	Sumerian	Egyptian	Hittite	Chinese
Man				
King				
Deity				
Ox				
Sheep				
Sky				
Star				
Sun				
Water				
Wood				
House				
Road				
City				
Land				

Pictorial signs from four ancient cultures compared.

origins of speech and script is characteristic of many ancient societies, that most peoples have myths which accept the magical identity of mythical representation and concrete reality and do not abstractly separate spoken and written communication. Extant texts from as early as 2700 BC verify that while Egyptian scribes revered the god Thoth as the patron of writing, they also associated the "master of papyrus" with the creative powers of divine speech: "The mighty Great One is Ptah, who transmitted [life to gods], as well as (to) their ka's, through his heart, by which Horus became Ptah, and through his tongue, by which Thoth became Ptah."

As creator of speech and writing, Thoth is also the administrative keeper of established order and protector against rebellion: "thou shalt be scribe there and keep in order those who are in them, *those who may perform deeds of rebellion...against me.*" Like Nabû, Thoth assumed certain calendrical and astronomical attributes of other gods. He was called the inventor of the arts and sciences as well as chronologer of the universe, for which reason he also became the god of the moon and is often artistically portrayed with a moon crescent. One of Thoth's most prominent functions is illustrated most memorably in the Book of the Dead, where he is portrayed as the scribe of truth and justice in the rite of the weighing of souls.

Other civilizations have produced their own myths about the origins of writing, ranging from Diodorus Siculus's account of Zeus's gift to the muses [Diodorus Siculus, *Bibliotheca historica*, V, 74.1–3, 1st century BC] to the Chinese legend of the four-eyed dragon god. Common to most of these early records, however, is the basic conviction that writing was sacred and of divine origins. And lest we try to restrict this notion to the earliest non-alphabetic systems of history, we need only consider the legendary accounts Bellamy presents in his chapter on ancient Arabic or the Koran, where Allah is named the creator of writing:

Read, in the name of thy Lord!
Who created man from congealed blood!
Read, for thy Lord is most generous!
Who taught the pen!
Taught man what he did not know!
(Sura 96.2–6)

Or, to take a more recent example, consider the native alphabet of the Far East, the Korean Han'gul. Han'gul was purportedly created by King Seijong (1417–50; and his palace scholars?) but was presented as having been born of divine origins: "It is the revelation of Heaven to the mind of the sage King to accomplish through his hand this great task and it is beyond the power of us, his subjects, to fully explain the wonders of its origins and essence."

At the nucleus of this vast array of mythical functions of the Egyptian and Sumerian as well as other deities of writing is a profound sense of the existential importance of writing to political power and order, to justice, and to the preservation of human life and to human destiny. The reverence which Middle Eastern cultures held for the religious and political values of written language represents one of the most immutable factors in the history of writing. Antiquity, as well as all literate societies since, recognized that with the invention of writing, words and ideas were no longer condemned to the brief fate of the spoken word or the short-lived memory of tradition.

Wayne M. Senner,
The Origins of Writing,
1989

Writing as a system of signs

Among the most famous of all abstract signs are the letters of the alphabet, which form other abstract signs, called words.

Ways of communicating ideas

A linguist examines the forms and structures of written communication, comparing it with gesture, voice, and other kinds of social expression.

The two most important external characteristics of human behaviour are expression and communication. The first affects what we may call personal behaviour, the second social behaviour.

Man has many ways, natural and artificial, of expressing his thoughts and his feelings. He can give expression in a natural way to his joy by laughing or humming and to his sorrow by weeping or moaning. He can express himself with the help of artificial means in a written poem, a painting, or any other piece of art. Man can try to communicate his feelings, thoughts, and ideas by means of conventional and generally understandable forms. What is the relation of expression to communication? Is there such a thing as pure expression or pure communication? Is it not rather that man, as a social being, …finds himself or visualizes himself to be at all times in conditions in which he can express himself only by communicating? And, vice versa, are not all the great masterpieces of art or poetry forms of communication achieved through the personal expression of individuals? It seems to me that the aims of expression and communication are so closely intertwined with each other in all forms of human behaviour that normally it is impossible to speak about one without being forced at the same time to consider the other.

In order to communicate thoughts and feelings there must be a conventional system of signs or symbols which, when used by some persons, are under-

stood by other persons receiving them. Communication under normal circumstances requires the presence of two (or more) persons, the one(s) who emit(s) and the one(s) who receive(s) the communication.

The process of communication is composed of two parts, emission and reception. As the means of emitting communication are too varied and numerous to allow for any systematic classification, our treatment must start from the point of view of reception. The reception of communication is achieved by means of our senses, of which sight, hearing, and touch play the most important roles. Theoretically, other senses, such as smell and taste, could also be taken into consideration, but in practice they play a very limited role and lead to no fully developed systems of signs.

Visual communication can be achieved by means of gesture and mimicry. Both are frequent companions

An Aztec codex written in 1554, after the Spanish Conquest, communicates with both Aztec pictograms and alphabetic text in Castilian Spanish.

of speech, although the intensity of their use differs with various individuals or social strata or folk groups. Some persons, more than others, use gesticulation or mimicry for oratorical effect or through natural impulse. In our society it is considered bad taste to 'talk with the hands'. It is a well-known fact that in Europe the southerners, like the Italians, use both gesticulation and mimicry to a much greater extent than, for instance, the Scandinavians or the British. A combination of language and gesture has played an important role in the ritual proceedings of all times and places. The restrictions imposed upon the use of language by natural and artificial conditions has resulted in the origin and development of systems of communication based on gesture and mimicry. Such are the systems developed for the use of deaf-mutes deprived by nature of the power of natural language. Here we may mention the gesture language of the Trappist monks, who, because of their vow of silence, were forced to develop a substitute system for speech. Systems of gesture language are often used among the Australian aborigines by widows who are not allowed to utter a word during the period of mourning. And, finally, the system of gesture language used among the Plains Indians was introduced as the need grew for communication between tribes speaking various mutually incomprehensible languages.

Among other ways of communication appealing to the eye we should mention optic signals by means of fire, smoke, light, semaphores, etc.

One of the simplest forms of auditory communication is, for instance, whistling with the intention of calling

someone. Hissing or applauding in the theatre are other simple specimens of this kind of communication. Sometimes artificial means, such as drums, whistles, or trumpets are used as acoustic signals.

The most important system of auditory communication is the spoken language directed to the ear of the person receiving the communication. Language is universal. Within the span of human knowledge there has never existed a group of men who have not possessed a fully developed language.

Simple ways of communicating feeling by the sense of touch are, for instance, the handclasp, the backslap, the lovestroke. A fully developed system of communication by handstroking is used among blind deaf-mutes, for which the best-known example is provided by the case of Helen Keller, the American writer and educator.

The[se] means of communication... have two features in common: (1) They are all of momentary value and are therefore restricted as to time; as soon as the word is uttered or the gesture made, it is gone and it cannot be revived except by repetition. (2) They can be used only in communication between persons more or less in proximity to each other and are therefore restricted as to space.

Above: Bronze Age (c. 2500–800 BC) pictographic rock drawings of two figures, Dumas cave, Ollioules, France, and, top, a large sun with rays ending in hands, from the Val Camonica, in the Italian Alps.

The need for finding a way to convey thoughts and feelings in a form not limited by time or space led to the development of methods of communication by means of (1) objects and (2) markings on objects or any solid material.

Visual means of communication with the help of objects are unlimited. When a person sets up a pile of stones or a single stone monument on a grave, he intends to give expression to his feelings for the deceased and to perpetuate his memory in the days to come. The cross symbolizing faith or the anchor symbolizing hope are further modern illustrations. A modern survival is the rosary, each bead of which, according to its position and size, is supposed to recall one certain prayer. We might also mention here the so-called "flower and gem languages," in which a certain flower or gem is supposed to convey a certain sentiment.

Systems of mnemonic signs to keep accounts by means of objects are known throughout the world.…

Writing is expressed not by objects themselves but by markings on objects or on any other material. Written symbols are normally executed by means of motor action of the hands in drawing, painting, scratching, or incising.…

The expressions just described give us illustrations for the mechanical background of writing, and at the same time point toward a very close connection between picture and writing. This is as it should be, since the most natural way of communicating ideas by means of visible markings is achieved by pictures. To the primitives a picture takes care in a crude way of the needs fulfilled in modern times by writing. In the course of time the picture develops in two directions: (1) pictorial art, in which pictures continue to reproduce more or less faithfully the objects and events of the surrounding world in a form independent of language; and (2) writing, in which signs, whether they retain their pictorial form or not, become ultimately secondary symbols for notions of linguistic value.…

The symbolism of visual images in the earliest stages of writing, like that of gesture signs, can express meaning without the necessity of a linguistic garment and both can profitably be investigated by a non-linguist. It is only after the development of writing into a full phonetic system, reproducing elements of speech, that we can speak of the practical identity of writing and speech and of epigraphy or paleography as being subdivisions of linguistics.

This tremendous difference between the *semasiographic* stage of writing (expressing meanings and notions

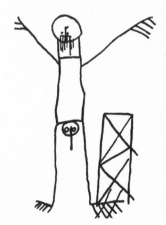

A Paleolithic figure of a bearded man, from the Sainte-Eulalie cave in the Ariège district of the French Pyrenees.

loosely connected with speech) and the *phonographic* stage (expressing speech) must be thoroughly emphasized here because of the controversies which are continuously taking place in the matter of the definition of writing. Those general linguists who define writing as a device for recording speech by means of visible marks, and take the written language to be a point-by-point equivalent of its spoken counterpart, show little appreciation of the historical development of writing and fail to see that such a definition cannot be applied to its early stages, in which writing only loosely expressed the spoken language. On the other hand, the philologists, who believe that writing even after the introduction of phonetization was used for the recording or transmission of both idea and sound, fail to understand that once man discovered a way of expressing exact forms of speech in written signs, writing lost its independent character and became largely a written substitute for its spoken counterpart....

FORERUNNERS OF WRITING
Descriptive-representational device
Among the forerunners of writing the most widely used class is that generally known by the misleading term of "pictographic" or "ideographic" writing. Such writing is best represented among the American Indians. Before entering into the difficult subject of definitions and terminology let us pause to glance at a few outstanding examples.

A simple communication of "no thoroughfare" was found in New Mexico on a rock drawing placed near a precipitous trail. The design warns horsemen that a mountain goat could

An American Indian rock drawing from New Mexico.

climb up the rocky trail but a horse would tumble down.

More complicated examples of transmission of communication by the American Indians are contained in the three following illustrations.

[This figure] represents a drawing, found on the face of a rock in Michigan

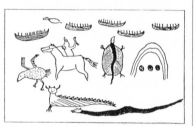

An American Indian rock drawing from Michigan.

on the shore of Lake Superior, which describes the course of a military expedition across the lake. At the top, five canoes carrying fifty-one men, represented by vertical strokes, can be seen. The expedition is led by a chieftain named Kishkemunasee, "Kingfisher," whose totem or animal symbol, in the form of a water bird, is drawn above the first canoe. The trip lasted three days, as we can judge from the pictures of three suns under three arches, representing the celestial dome. After a happy landing, symbolized by the picture of a turtle, the expedition marched on quickly, as can be seen from the picture of a man riding a horse. The eagle, symbol of courage, embodies the spirit of the warriors. The description closes with pictures of a panther and a serpent, the symbols of force and cunning respectively, whom the chief invokes for help in the military expedition.

[Next] is a letter sent by mail from a Southern Cheyenne, named Turtle-Following-His-Wife, at the Cheyenne and Arapaho Agency, Indian Territory, to his son, Little-Man, at the Pine Ridge Agency, Dakota. It was drawn on a half-sheet of ordinary writing paper, without a word written, and was enclosed in an envelope, which was addressed to "Little-Man, Cheyenne, Pine Ridge Agency," in the ordinary manner, written by someone at the first-named

agency. The letter was evidently understood by Little-Man as he immediately called upon Dr. V. T. McGillycuddy, Indian agent at Pine Ridge Agency, and was aware that the sum of $53 had been placed to his credit for the purpose of enabling him to pay his expenses in going the long journey to his father's home in Indian Territory. Dr. McGilly-cuddy had, by the same mail, received a letter from Agent Dyer, enclosing $53, and explaining the reason for its being sent, which enabled him also to understand the pictographic letter. With the above explanation it very clearly shows, over the head of the figure to the left, the turtle following the turtle's wife united with the head of a figure by a line, and over the head of the other figure, also united by a line to it, is a little man. Also over the right arm of the last-

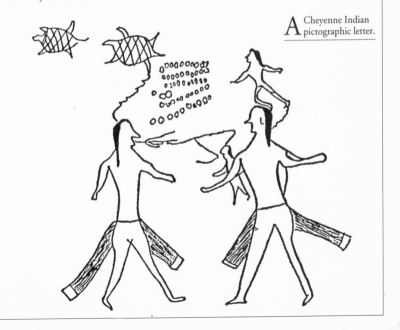

A Cheyenne Indian pictographic letter.

A letter from an Ojibwa girl to her lover.

mentioned figure is another little man in the act of springing or advancing toward Turtle-Following-His-Wife, from whose mouth proceed two lines, curved or hooked at the end, as if drawing the little figure towards him. It is suggested that the last-mentioned part of the pictograph is the substance of the communication, i.e. "come to me," the larger figures with their name totems being the persons addressed and addressing. Between and above the two large figures are fifty-three round objects intended for dollars. Both the Indian figures have on breechcloths, corresponding with the information given concerning them, which is that they are Cheyennes....

[Next] is a letter written by an Ojibwa girl to a favoured lover, requesting him to call at her lodge. The girl is represented by the bear totem, the boy by that of the mud puppy. The trail leads toward the lakes, shown by the three irregular circles, whence it branches off in the direction of two tents. Three Christian girls, indicated by the crosses, are encamped there. From one of the tents protrudes the arm of the girl inviting the Indian boy to call on her. Observe that this drawing has some of the characteristic features of a map, such as the trail and the lakes, side by side with such symbolic representations as the protruding hand expressing the idea of invitation.

Communication can sometimes be adequately expressed by means of a sequence of simple drawings in a manner which the Germans call... "continuous illustration." In modern times good examples for this device are wordless comic strips....While one picture in a cartoon is *per se* understandable, the meaning is conveyed only by the sequence of all the pictures in a certain order.

I. J. Gelb,
A Study of Writing,
rev. ed., 1963

A West African writing tradition

In the modern era an esoteric African sign system preserves secrecy and power.

The ideographs of the Ejagham people of southwestern Cameroon and southeastern Nigeria explode the myth of Africa as a continent without a tradition of writing. The Ejagham developed a unique form of ideographic writing, signs representing ideas and called *nsibidi,* signs embodying many powers, including the essence of all that is valiant, just, and ordered.

Numerous Ejagham women and men in traditional institutions—"the whole country is honeycombed with secret societies," an English explorer observed early in the twentieth century—wear ritual dress and make gestures strongly influenced by the patterns of *nsibidi,* extending the reach and complexity of Ejagham traditional writing. Titled elders in major institutions (Nnimm, Eja, Ngbe) establish power or prestige by mastering arcane signs of sacred

Dogon drummers from Mali: the drum is both musical instrument and communication device.

presence and recollection, luminous ciphers of the founding rulers and most important women. The force of *nsibidi* is a mystery. Some traditional Ejagham continue to regard this mystery as rationale governing their lives and labor.

Nsibidi, in the Ejagham language, means roughly "cruel letters." *Sibidi* means "cruel" in classical Ejagham, according to Peter Eno of Mamfe, Cameroon, and authority on the art and language of his people. P. Amaury Talbot, an English author, discovered while traveling through Ejagham country that *sibi* meant "bloodthirsty." Consider *nsibidi* writing, then, as justifiable terror in the service of law and government. As might be expected, the traditional executioner society— men who killed convicted murderers or launched peremptory strikes against outside enemies—was called the Nsibidi Society.

Few see the richest and most awesome of the signs of the *nsibidi* corpus, the intricate diagrams drawn upon the ground to control a crisis or honor the funeral of a very important person. As Peter Eno remarks: "*Nsibidi* signs represent the heart, the very depth of our ancient Ejagham societies, showing the last stage, the final rites, and only the core of the members can come out to view such signs." Ejagham ideographic writing both exalts the power of privileged persons and points to a universe of aesthetic and intellectual potentiality. Poetic play and stylized valor, artistic battles of mime and "action writing" enliven, with pleasure and improvisation, the dark dimensions of *nsibidi.*

Nsibidi do not derive from Western writing systems. There are no Arabic or Latin letters in the script. It is wholly African. The invocation of divine beginnings occasions the writing of certain of the most important signs, even as does the centering of power upon a seat of final justice. The moral and civilizing impact of *nsibidi* betrays the ethnocentrism of an ideology that would exclude ideographic forms from consideration in the history of literacy. Educated Western persons continue to assume that black traditional Africa was culturally impoverished because it lacked letters to record its central myths, ideals, and aspirations. Yet the Ejagham and Ejagham-influenced blacks who elaborated a creole offshoot of *nsibidi* in Cuba have proven otherwise.

Ejagham and Ejagham-influenced captives arrived in western Cuba primarily during the first four decades of the nineteenth century, as a result of the immense rise in sugar cultivation in that portion of the island. The slaves included members of the all-important male "leopard society," called Ngbe in Ejagham. These men founded their own "society," promulgating Ngbe values of nobility and government and remembering the master metaphor of masculine accomplishment, the leopard, who moves with perfect elegance and strength. Ngbe in Cuba was known by the creole name, Abakuá, after Abakpa, a term by which the Ejagham of Calabar are designated.

Nsibidi signs emerged in Cuba no later than 1839, when the archives of the police of Havana received confiscated papers from a black man's raided premises, papers emblazoned with Ejagham-influenced ideographs, signatures of high-ranking Abakuá priests. The sacred signs and signatures of Cuban Abakuá are chiefly called *anaforuana,* among other names. More than five hundred signs have emerged among the blacks of the traditional barrios of six cities in western Cuba: Marianao, Havana, Guanabacoa, Regla, Cárdenas, and Matanzas. Most of these ideographs are hypnotic variants of a leitmotif of mystic vision: four eyes, two worlds, God the Father—the fish, the king—and the Efut princess who in death became his bride. These signs are written and rewritten with mantraic power and pulsation. Mediatory forces, the sacred signs of the *anaforuana* corpus, indicate a realm beyond ordinary discourse. They are calligraphic gestures of erudition and black grandeur, spiritual presences traced in yellow or white chalk (yellow for life, white for death) on the ground of inner patios or on the floor of sacred rooms, bringing back the spirit of departed ancestors, describing the proprieties of initiation and funereal leave-taking.

Robert Farris Thompson,
*Flash of the Spirit:
African and Afro-American
Art and Philosophy,*
1983

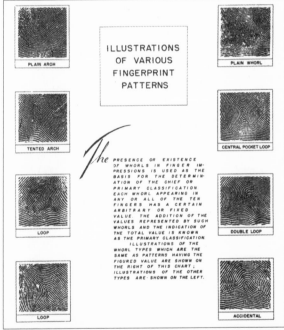

ILLUSTRATIONS OF VARIOUS FINGERPRINT PATTERNS

PLAIN ARCH

PLAIN WHORL

TENTED ARCH

CENTRAL POCKET LOOP

The PRESENCE OR EXISTENCE OF WHORLS IN FINGER IMPRESSIONS IS USED AS THE BASIS FOR THE DETERMINATION OF THE CHIEF OR PRIMARY CLASSIFICATION EACH WHORL APPEARING IN ANY OR ALL OF THE TEN FINGERS HAS A CERTAIN ARBITRARY OR FIXED VALUE. THE ADDITION OF THE VALUES REPRESENTED BY SUCH WHORLS AND THE INDICATION OF THE TOTAL VALUE IS KNOWN AS THE PRIMARY CLASSIFICATION. ILLUSTRATIONS OF THE WHORL TYPES WHICH ARE THE SAME AS PATTERNS HAVING THE FIGURED VALUE ARE SHOWN ON THE RIGHT OF THIS CHART; ILLUSTRATIONS OF THE OTHER TYPES ARE SHOWN ON THE LEFT.

LOOP

DOUBLE LOOP

LOOP

ACCIDENTAL

At birth each of us is given a name, a personal identity label. But we bear, inscribed in the very cells of our bodies, identification markers far more uniquely individual than any written or spoken name tag: DNA codes, at the genetic level, and the visible signs of our fingerprints. Such physical "signatures" are extremely useful in both medical research and law enforcement. Above: basic forms of fingerprint classification from the United States Federal Bureau of Investigation, c. 1960.

Styles of mapping

*Maps and diagrams ancient
and modern represent the world
—or some aspect of it—in a
variety of stylized ways. Here are
some very different examples.*

Symbols may be placed on maps to relate
quantitative data to appropriate geographical areas. This 1935 Dutch statistical survey
map indicates quantities of oil, sugar, grain,
corn, and coffee exported from various Latin
American countries.

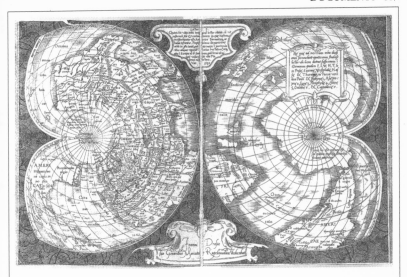

G erard Mercator (1512–94), *Orbis imago,* published in Louvain, Flanders, in 1538, is the first
world map to identify North and South America, and is also an elegant graphic design.

T his chart was extremely innovative in its time. Drawn by Charles Joseph Minard in 1869, it
uses graphic techniques to describe the disastrous advance of Napoleon's army on Moscow in
the Russian campaign of 1812–13. Data indicate the changes in the weather, the progressive loss of
troops, and the territory covered.

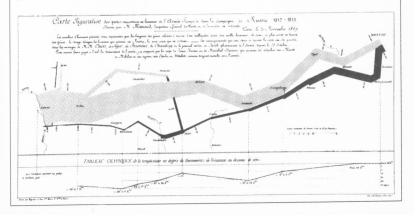

Kāshgarlī Mahmūd, a map from the *Diwan-i Lughat al-Turk,* a 9th–15th century Turkish manuscript.

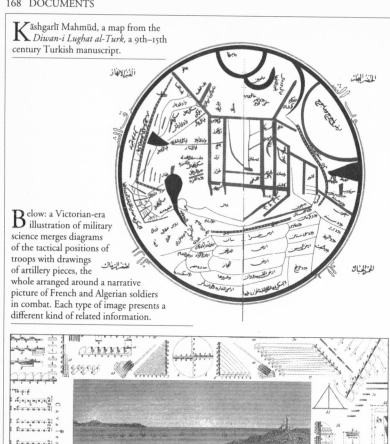

Below: a Victorian-era illustration of military science merges diagrams of the tactical positions of troops with drawings of artillery pieces, the whole arranged around a narrative picture of French and Algerian soldiers in combat. Each type of image presents a different kind of related information.

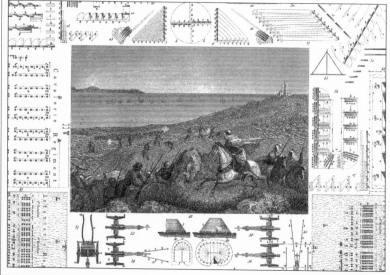

This clay tablet from c. 1300 BC is a map of irrigation canals on a royal estate near Nippur, in Mesopotamia. The circles indicate villages.

Below: this 19th-century map of the Italian port city of Ancona combines a flat, schematic urban street plan with a topographic description of hills, cliffs, and water.

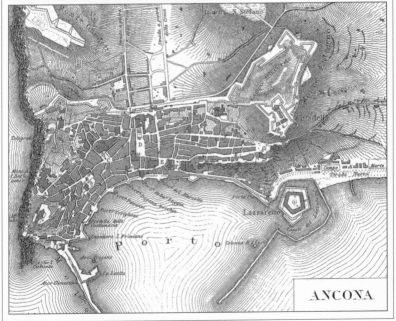

ANCONA

Codes, signals, body language

Words and pictures are but two categories of communicative signs. Others serve a variety of purposes.

Long-distance signals

Beacon fires were the ancient forerunners of the telegraph, carrying urgent messages over vast spans of territory. In this scene from an early classical Greek play, the queen of Argos describes receiving the news of her husband's victory in the Trojan War, and names the beacon-bearing mountains that run from Troy, in northern Turkey, to Argos, in southern Greece.

CHORUS: How long then, is it since the
    citadel was stormed?
CLYTAEMESTRA: It is the night, the
    mother of this dawn I hailed.
CHORUS: What kind of messenger
    could come in speed like this?
CLYTAEMESTRA: Hephaestus, who cast
    forth the shining blaze from Ida.
And beacon after beacon picking up
    the flare
carried it here; Ida to the Hermaean
    horn
of Lemnos, where it shone above the
    isle, and next
the sheer rock face of Zeus on Athos
    caught it up;
and plunging skyward to arch the
    shoulders of the sea
the strength of the running flare in
    exultation,

A selection of royal and national flags, c. 1851.

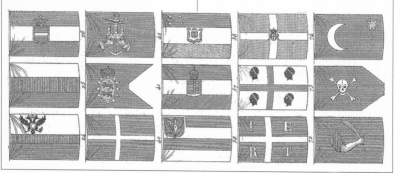

pine timbers flaming into gold, like the sunrise,
brought the bright message to Macistus' sentinel cliffs,
who, never slow nor in the carelessness of sleep
caught up, sent on his relay in the courier chain,
and far across Euripus' streams the beacon fire
carried to signal watchmen on Messapion.
These took it again in turn, and heaping high a pile
of silvery brush flamed it to throw the message on.
And the flare sickened never, but grown stronger yet
outleapt the river valley of Asopus like
the very moon for shining, to Cithaeron's scaur
to waken the next station of the flaming post.
These watchers, not contemptuous of the far-thrown blaze,
kindled another beacon vaster than commanded.
The light leaned high above Gorgopis' staring marsh,
and striking Aegyplanctus' mountain

The American frigate *USS Constitution,* moored at Malta in 1837, marks the birthday of George Washington by flying her colors—that is, displaying all her flags.

top, drove on
yet one more relay, lest the flare die down in speed.
Kindled once more with stintless heaping force, they send
the beard of flame to hugeness, passing far beyond
the promontory that gazes on the Saronic strait
and flaming far, until it plunged at last to strike
the steep rock of Arachnus near at hand, our watchtower.
And thence there fell upon this house of Atreus' sons
the flare whose fathers mount to the Idaean beacon.
These are the changes on my torchlight messengers,
one from another running out the laps assigned.
The first and the last sprinters have the victory.
By such proof and such symbol I announce to you

my lord at Troy has sent his messengers
to me.

Aeschylus, *Agamemnon*,
ll. 278–316, c. 458 BC,
translated by Richmond Lattimore,
1942

A rude Renaissance gesture

*The body speaks through gesture, pose, and
expression. A glance may offend or flatter;
a twitch of the hand may support or
contradict a spoken comment. The quar-
reling Capulet and Montague families of
Shakespeare's* Romeo and Juliet *knew
quite well how to use vulgar and offensive
facial expressions and hand gestures to
provoke one another whenever they met.*

GREGORY: I will frown as I pass by,
and let them take it as they list.
SAMPSON: Nay, as they dare. I will bite
my thumb at them; which is a
disgrace to them, if they bear it.
ABRAHAM: Do you bite your thumb at
us, sir?
SAMPSON: I do bite my thumb, sir.
ABRAHAM: Do you bite your thumb at
us, sir?
SAMPSON: (*Aside to Gregory*) Is the law
of our side if I say ay?
GREGORY: (*Aside to Sampson*) No.
SAMPSON: No, sir, I do not bite my
thumb at you, sir; but I bite my
thumb, sir.
GREGORY: Do you quarrel, sir?
ABRAHAM: Quarrel, sir! no, sir.
SAMPSON: If you do, sir, I am for
you… [*They fight*]

William Shakespeare,
Romeo and Juliet, I.i,
c. 1594–95

Gestures in the theater

*The Nobel Prize–winning Italian actor
and director Dario Fo has long studied*

*the traditional theatrical practices of
mime, dance, and movement, and has
evolved precise theories about their origins
and communicative functions.*

MATCHING TRADE AND GESTURE
…[Georgi Valentinovich Plekhanov
(1857–1918), Russian Marxist philosopher, author of *Art & Social Life*]
believed that the style of gesture of
every people derives from its relationship with the need to survive. A very
great researcher, a Russian anthropologist…[he] had, from his studies into
the gestures of hundreds of different
peoples, discovered that the rhythm

Opposite: In 1872 Charles Darwin published a scientific study that attempted to establish a taxonomy of facial expressions, *The Expression of the Emotions in Man and Animals*. It was illustrated with posed photographs. Above: surprise, photographed by Oscar Gustave Reijlander; below: fright, by Dr. Guillaume Benjamin Duchenne de Boulogne.

and timing of the essential acts in the performance of jobs or trades indispensable for survival determine the general contours of human behaviour. They are responsible for the general attitude which is then applied in other areas that could be considered accessory to life, such as dancing, singing, playing. All these activities are linked by the style in which they are conducted to the basic occupation practised to earn a livelihood....

Decroux, the great French master of mime, has a display of different styles of walk which lasts for no less than three-quarters of an hour. Each one of us has an individual gait. I am aware that I have a very unusual way of walking, a cross between a horse and a flamingo. Everybody should get to know their own walk and basic gestures....

Once I was giving a lecture at a conference on the relationship between audience and production. I decided to improvise and went on to the platform and gave imitations of all the speakers who had preceded me....I showed up the varying peculiarities and all the different ways of pointing fingers, waving arms, leaning forward with head and shoulders. One man sawed the air with broad strokes, another built up piles of odd-shaped volumes; there was yet another who fought out a private duel with one hand, only to stop suddenly and flutter the other about, finally free and at peace.

The odd thing was that none of the caricatures was recognised by the subject himself! 'No, I don't do that!' All the rest immediately chorused: 'It's you to a T!' They grinned while the victim looked around in amazement. The fact is that we are blithely unaware of the gestures we ourselves produce. We read our words, we are careful about our pronunciation, and would be enraged with ourselves if we were to split an infinitive or misplace a pronoun. On the other hand, we are indifferent about the gestures that accompany our speech, even though they could be every bit as coarse, inelegant or uncouth. How is this to be explained? What makes us believe that gestures and movements are the side dish, the salad, while the word is the main course, the meat? This notion has been inculcated into us all since our schooldays. Ever since nursery, the pronunciation of each and every word will have been corrected, but no one will ever have bothered about the accompanying gesture. By the same

Krishna Dancing, an 18th-century Nepalese votive statue.

token, gestures have been relegated to a secondary position in the actor's vocabulary....

GENEROUS AND PETTY GESTURES
There are thousands of conventional gestures which in day-to-day speech are used to facilitate communication. To rub your hand on your stomach, as everyone knows, indicates anticipation of a delicious meal. In Italy, these signs are more numerous, so that running your thumb down the cheek indicates someone who is sharp and a bit sly, whereas pulling down the skin under the eye means open your eyes, smarten up! Resting the cheek against one hand and leaning your head slightly conveys the information that you are tired, and so on. The mime must completely ignore signs of this sort, precisely because they are banal, well-worn stereotypes and do not indicate the presence of intelligent imagination. Any actor who made use of them to express sleep or hunger would be the poorest of performers, because in theatre it is as essential to re-invent gestures as it is to re-invent words.

It is important to begin from reality and not from the conventions of reality....

In a famous work of kabuki theatre, the actor who plays the character of the fox mimes the animal—its prowl, its tail wagging, its crouch—all without ever actually stretching out on the ground. He never goes down on all fours and never even needs to bend his back. It is sufficient for him to wave his arm in a certain way to make you aware that that is his tail. He turns his head to one side, swings round the other, darts his eyes and holds them in the one spot and you have a fox to a T, even for someone who has never seen a fox in his life. The act portrays all the wiles and cunning, and when he speaks, the voice is that of a hypocritical and unreliable being. Behind this display there lies a choice, a moral choice. I might almost say that in addition a certain political value is given. An ideological presupposition stands at the root of the whole story, and this choice

A young lady waves goodbye ("*Auf Wiederseh'n!*") at a German railway station in 1925. What is the meaning of her smile? Is she glad to be parting from the person she salutes? Is she delighted to be leaving?

The classical music conductor Herbert von Karajan at work in Salzburg in 1968. Unable to speak during the performance, a conductor directs the orchestra with a set of highly formal prescribed gestures.

conditions the manner of styling the gestures, the synthesis, the rhythms and the cadences.

Dario Fo,
Tricks of the Trade, 1987,
translated by Joe Farrell, 1991

Japanese traditional theater

Japanese culture has developed a number of performance arts that rely on stylized masks, poses, and gestures to convey precise, often highly poetic meanings. Among these are Kabuki theater, Butoh puppetry, the martial arts of karate and aikido, and the exquisite stage style called Noh.

All imaginative art keeps at a distance and this distance once chosen must be firmly held against a pushing world. Verse, ritual, music and dance in association with action require that gesture, costume, facial expression, stage arrangement must help in keeping the door. Our unimaginative arts are content to set a piece of the world as we know it in a place by itself, to put their photographs as it were in a plush or a

1. Pataka   2. Mudrakya   3. Kataka   4. Mushti   5. Kartari Mukha   6. Sukutundam

plain frame, but the arts which interest me, while seeming to separate from the world and us a group of figures, images, symbols, enable us to pass for a few moments into a deep of the mind that had hitherto been too subtle for our habitation. As a deep of the mind can only be approached through what is most human, most delicate, we should distrust bodily distance, mechanism and loud noise. It may be well if we go to school in Asia, for the distance from life in European art has come from little but difficulty with material....

Therefore it is natural that I go to Asia for a stage-convention, for more formal faces, for a chorus that has no part in the action and perhaps for those movements of the body copied from the marionette shows of the fourteenth century. A mask will enable me to substitute for the face of some commonplace player, or for that face repainted to suit his own vulgar fancy, the fine invention of a sculptor, and to bring the audience close enough to the play to hear every inflection of the voice. A mask never seems but a dirty

face, and no matter how close you go is still a work of art; nor shall we lose by staying the movement of the features, for deep feeling is expressed by a movement of the whole body....

> Ezra Pound and
> Ernest Fenellosa,
> *The Classic Noh Theatre*
> *of Japan,*
> 1959

The visual language of the deaf

Among the most beautiful and eloquent languages is that used by deaf people, which literally incorporates, or embodies, words in movements of the hands, face, and body. Here a research neurologist explores the formal structures and rhythms of the language called Sign.

[Sign satisfies] every linguistic criterion of a genuine language, in its lexicon and syntax, its capacity to generate an infinite number of propositions. In 1960 [William] Stokoe published *Sign Language Structure....*Stokoe was convinced that signs were *not* pictures, but complex abstract symbols with a complex inner structure. He was the

7. Kapitha   8. Hamsapaksha   9. Sikharam   10. Hamsasyam   11. Anjali   12. Ardha-Chandra

13. Mukuram   **14. Bhramara**   **15. Suchi**   **16. Pallava**   **17. Tri-pataka**   **18. Mriga Sirsa**

first, then, to look for a structure, to analyze signs, to dissect them, to search for constituent parts. Very early he proposed that each sign had at least three independent parts—location, handshape, and movement (analogous to the phonemes of speech)—and that each part had a limited number of combinations. In *Sign Language Structure* he delineated nineteen different handshapes, twelve locations, twenty-four types of movements, and invented a notation for these—American Sign Language had never been *written* before. His *Dictionary* was equally original, for the signs were arranged not thematically (e.g. signs for food, signs for animals, etc.) but systematically, according to their parts, and organization, and principles of the language. It showed the lexical structure of the language—the linguistic interrelatedness of a basic three thousand sign "words."...

This marvelous organic structure—the intricate embryo of grammar—[can] exist in a purely visual form, and [does] so in Sign....

It was evident that the bare lexicon

The twenty-four *hastas,* symbolic hand positions in the Kathakali dance tradition of India.

of the *Dictionary of American Sign* was only a first step—for a language is not just a lexicon or code. (Indian sign language, so-called, is a mere code—i.e., a collection or vocabulary of signs, the signs themselves having no internal structure and scarcely capable of being modified grammatically.) A genuine language is continually modulated by grammatical and syntactic devices of all sorts. There is an extraordinary richness of such devices in ASL, which serve to amplify the basic vocabulary hugely....The face may also serve special, linguistic functions in Sign: thus specific facial expressions, or, rather "behaviors," may serve to mark syntactic constructions such as topics, relative clauses, and questions, or function as adverbs or quantifiers. Other parts of the body may also be involved. Any or all of this—this vast range of actual or potential inflections, spatial and kinetic—can converge upon the root signs, fuse with them,

19. Sarpa Sirsa   **20. Vardhamana**   **21. Arala**   **22. Urnanabha**   **23. Mukula**   **24. Kataka Mukha**

and modify them, compacting an enormous amount of information into the resulting signs.

It is the *compression* of these sign units, and the fact that all their modifications are *spatial,* that makes Sign, at the obvious and visible level, completely unlike any spoken language, and which, in part, prevented it from being seen as a language at all. But it is precisely this, along with its unique spatial syntax and grammar, which marks Sign as a true language—albeit a completely novel one, out of the evolutionary mainstream of all spoken languages, a unique evolutionary alternative. (And, in a way, a completely surprising one, considering we have become specialized for speech in the last half million or two million years. The potentials for language are in us all—this is easy to understand. But that the potentials are a *visual* language mode should also be so great—this is astonishing, and would hardly be anticipated if visual language did not actually occur. But, equally, it might be said that making signs and gestures, albeit without complex linguistic structure, goes back to our remote, prehuman past—and that speech is really the evolutionary newcomer; a highly successful newcomer which could replace the hands, freeing them for other, non-communicational purposes. Perhaps, indeed, there have been two parallel evolutionary streams for spoken and signed forms of language: this is suggested by the work of certain anthropologists, who have shown the co-existence of spoken and signed languages in some primitive tribes. Thus the deaf, and their language, show us not only the plasticity but the latent potentials of the nervous system.)

The single most remarkable feature of Sign—that which distinguishes it from all other languages and mental activities—is its unique linguistic use of space. The complexity of this linguistic space is quite overwhelming for the "normal" eye, which cannot see, let alone understand, the sheer intricacy of its spatial patterns.

We see then, in Sign, at every level—lexical, grammatical, syntactic—a *linguistic* use of space: a use that is amazingly complex, for much of what occurs linearly, sequentially, temporally in speech, becomes simultaneous, concurrent, multileveled in Sign. The "surface" of Sign may appear simple to the eye, like that of gesture or mime, but one soon finds that this is an illusion, and what looks so simple is extraordinarily complex and consists of innumerable spatial patterns nested, three-dimensionally, in each other.

Oliver Sacks,
Seeing Voices: A Journey into the World of the Deaf,
1989

The unpronounced name, written in icon form, of the popular musician and artist formerly known as Prince abandons verbal language entirely, in favor of the pure visual symbol.

Motifs from ancient art display the use of symbolic gestures, whose meaning we may only guess at today. Left to right: a Chinese thunder god; an Inca god of air, from Peru; Diana of Ephesus, a fertility goddess originally from Asia Minor; Set, Egyptian god of war; Marduk, the Babylonian creator god.

The world of symbols

The word symbol *derives from the ancient Greek* symbolon, *a token composed of two halves, used to verify identity by matching one part to the other. It has come to mean a concrete sign or image that represents some other, more abstract thing or idea by convention, analogy, or metaphor.*

Origin and continuity of the symbol

The early historical record is laden with symbolic images and objects whose meaning we can only guess at today. Numerology, the gods, the calendar, the rhythms of agriculture and society—all these are sources of the rich symbolism of human history.

The symbol is a vehicle at once universal and particular. Universal, since it transcends history; particular, because it relates to a definite period of history. Without going into questions of 'origin', we shall show that most writers agree in tracing the beginnings of symbolist thought to prehistoric times—to the latter part of the Palaeolithic Age.... The process whereby the beings of this world are ordered according to their properties, so that the words of action and of spiritual and moral facts may be explored by analogy, is one which can also be seen, with the dawning of history, in the transition of the pictograph into the ideograph, as well as in the origins of art.

We could adduce an immense weight

of testimony offered by human faith and wisdom proving that the invisible or spiritual order is analogous to the material order. We shall come back to this later when we define 'analogy'. Let us recall the saying of Plato, taken up later by the pseudo-Dionysius the Areopagite: 'What is perceptible to the senses is the reflection of what is intelligible to the mind'; and echoed in the *Tabula Smaragdina*: 'What is below is like what is above; what is above is like what is below', and also in the remark of Goethe: 'What is within is also without.' However it may be, symbolism is organized in its vast explanatory and creative function as a system of highly complex relations, one in which the dominant factor is always a polarity, linking the physical and metaphysical worlds. What Palaeolithic Man evolved out of this process is impossible to know except through indirect deductions. Our knowledge about the latter part of the neolithic age is considerably wider. Schneider and Berthelot both consider that this was the period (that is: possibly the fourth millenary before

Detail of an American $1.00 bill, showing the Great Seal of the United States, designed in 1782, with its symbols of the unfinished pyramid and Eye of Providence.

Opposite: *God Sees Me:* a 19th-century religious image from Flanders displays the Eye of God and the dove of the Holy Spirit.

history) when man underwent that great transformation which endowed him with the gifts of creation and organization, qualities which distinguish him from the merely natural world. Berthelot, who has studied this process in the Near East, has given the name of 'astrobiology' to the religious and intellectual cultures of that epoch.

The evolution of Man up to this point in history must have passed through the following stages: animism; totemism; and megalithic, lunar and solar cultures. The subsequent stages must have been: cosmic ritualism; polytheism; monotheism; and, finally, moral philosophy. Berthelot considers astrology, astronomy, arithmetic and alchemy of Chaldean origin....

He defines…"astrobiology" [as] the interplay of astronomic law (the mathematical order) and vegetable and animal life (the biological order). All things form at one and the same time an organic whole and a precise order.... [Agriculture] ensures an appreciation of their annual "rhythm" of growth, flowering, fructifying, sowing and harvesting, a rhythm which is in direct and constant relation to the calendar, in other words, the position of the

Risk of grounding

heavenly bodies. Time and natural phenomena were measured by reference to the moon before they came to be measured by the sun....Astrobiology hovers between a biology of the heavenly bodies and an astronomy of human beings; beginning with the former, it tends towards the latter'. During the neolithic era the geometric idea of space was formulated; so also were the significance of the number seven (derived from this concept of space), the relation between heaven and earth, the cardinal points, and the relations between the various elements of the septenary (the planetary gods, the days of the week) and between those of the quaternary (the seasons, the colours, the cardinal points, the elements)....

The argument about whether European megalithic culture came before or after the great oriental civilizations is far from settled. Here questions of symbolism arise. The importance of the Franco-Cantabrian zone in the Palaeolithic age is well known; it is also known that the art forms of this district spread across Europe in the direction of Siberia and southwards across North Africa to the southernmost part of the continent. There was, no doubt, a period of transition between this early flowering and the great megalithic monuments. ...[Schneider] points out that there are marked similarities between the ideas of regions as far apart as America, New Guinea, Indonesia, Western Europe, Central Asia and the Far East, that is to say, of areas in all parts of the world.

Let us consider now the similarity between the discoveries attributed by Schneider to megalithic European culture and those ascribed by Berthelot

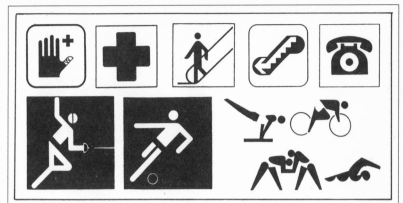

to the Far East. In Schneider's opinion the final stage of neolithic development differed from the earlier stage 'in the preference it showed for static and geometric forms, in its organizing and creative genius (evolving fabulous animals, musical instruments, mathematical proportions, number-ideas, astronomy and a tonal system with truly musical sounds). The carrying over of totemistic mystical elements into a more advanced, pastoral civilization explains some of the fundamental characteristics of the new mystique....The entire cosmos comes to be conceived after the human pattern. As the essence of all phenomena is, in the last resort, a vibrant rhythm, the intimate nature of phenomena is directly perceptible by polyrhythmic human consciousness. For this reason, imitating is knowing. The echo is the paradigmatic form of imitation. Language, geometric symbols and number-ideas are a cruder form of imitation.' Schneider then observes that according to Speiser and Heine-Geldern, 'the outstanding cultural elements of megalithic culture are: cyclopean buildings, commemo-

Modern pictographs include, opposite, English road signs and, above, American public-information signs.

rative stones, stones as the dwelling-places of souls, cultural stone-circles, *palafittes,* head-hunting, the sacrifice of oxen, eye-shaped ornaments, death-ships, family-trees, signal-drums, the sacrificial stake, and labyrinths'.

It is precisely these elements that have most successfully preserved their symbolic form down the ages. And did not these express, even in megalithic times, the very essence of human life, bursting from the unconscious in the shape of a constructive and configurating longing? Or was it, rather, the ever-present, primary forms of life, sacrifice and intellection of the world which found everlasting expression in these cultural creations, making an ineradicable impression on the mind of Man? One may unhesitatingly answer in the affirmative to both questions, for they refer to the different but parallel phenomena of culture and psychology.

J. E. Cirlot,
A Dictionary of Symbols,
1962, translated by Jack Sage

Religious symbols

Many religious writers and artists convey their core ideas of the ineffable and spiritual through symbols, finding the language of literal description inadequate. Here, a Christian writer examines his religion's use of symbols.

The Christian asserts that man is created in the image of God. He declares that God has given man a soul, capable of reaching up into Heaven itself and inspiring the human mind to its noblest achievement, the quest after God.

It is this spiritual aspiration that lifts man to his greatest heights. No words have ever been found that are adequate to give it satisfactory expression…. [But] there is a language for these experiences…. It is called the language of the sign and the symbol, the outward

and visible form through which is revealed the inward and invisible reality that moves and directs the soul…. Because the experiences of the soul with

life's deepest realities are made known through them, they are a truly universal language. These signs and symbols are the language of the soul….

In common practice they are used interchangeably. A sign is a symbol; a symbol is a sign. However, without becoming technical, there is a distinction that should be made between them which may be of assistance. A sign *represents*. It points to something, and takes its character from what is done with it. The cross represents the Christian faith and points to Christ's

Crucifixion. A symbol *resembles*. It has acquired a deeper meaning than the sign, because it is more completely identified with what it represents, and its character is derived from what is known by it. The lamb, the sacrificial animal of the Jewish faith, was offered upon the altar as a propitiation for sin. Christ was

Above left: Christian symbols of God include the Greek cross, with branches of equal length, and the eternal circle, whose end is its beginning; left: the monogram of Jesus, surmounted by a cross, has several interpretations: *JHS* are the first three letters of the name in Greek; in Latin the initials may stand for *In Hoc Signo,* in this sign, or *Jesus Hominum Salvator,* Jesus redeemer of humankind; above: three North American Indian symbols of the sun.

identified as the Lamb of God because the offering of Himself upon the Cross resembled this act of atonement. The Cross symbolizes God's love for man in the sacrifice of His Son for the sins of the world....

Christian man, in his quest after God, attaches to well-known words, actions, or things, a mystical and spiritual meaning. In this manner divine truth is recognized and a deeper insight is given to man's ability to understand God's presence in all creation. It was because the Christian Church believed the Christ to be the Saviour of all men that she used the universal language of the sign and the symbol. She was convinced that it was her task to redeem the world, and

all men, under God's plan as it was now revealed in His Son. Therefore, she did not hesitate to borrow from every available source in her effort to further this commission. The sign and the symbol, particularly those most common in the realm of human experience, were given a Christian and spiritual meaning....

The early Christian saw God in everything. In God he 'lived and moved and had his being.' It followed quite naturally that, in his eyes, everything was symbolical of God.

George Ferguson,
*Signs and Symbols in
Christian Art,*
1954

Armorial bearings of the kingdom of Spain in a 19th-century illustration.

Reading visual signs

Maps, charts, diagrams—these complex sign systems, so different from written languages, may also sometimes require translation.

What a map tells us

A map comprises a set of universally understood signs…or does it?

MAPS FOR POLITICAL PROPAGANDA

A good propagandist knows how to shape opinion by manipulating maps. Political persuasion often concerns territorial claims, nationalities, national pride, borders, strategic positions, conquests, attacks, troop movements, defenses, spheres of influence, regional inequality, and other geographic phenomena conveniently portrayed cartographically. The propagandist molds the map's message by emphasizing supporting features, suppressing contradictory information, and choosing provocative, dramatic symbols. People trust maps, and intriguing maps attract the eye as well as connote authority. Naive citizens willingly accept as truth maps based on a biased and sometimes fraudulent selection of facts.

Although all three manipulate opinion, the propagandist's goals differ from those of the advertiser and the real-estate developer. Both the advertiser and the political propagandist attempt to generate demand, but the advertiser sells a product or service, not an ideology. Both the advertiser and the propagandist attempt to lower public resistance or to improve a vague or tarnished image, but the advertiser's objectives are commercial and financial, whereas the propagandist's are diplomatic and military. Both the real-estate developer and the political propagandist seek approval or permission, but the developer is concerned with a much smaller territory, often uninhabited, and seldom acts unilaterally without official sanction. Although both the real-estate developer and the propagandist face

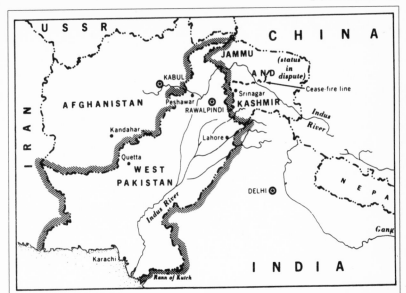

The disputed India–Pakistan boundary and the territory of Jammu and Kashmir, as portrayed in the 1965 *Area Handbook for Pakistan,* published by the United States government.

opponents, the developer usually confronts groups of neighboring property owners, environmentalists, or historic preservationists, whereas the propagandist commonly confronts a vocal ethnic minority, another country, an alliance of countries, an opposing ideology, or a widely accepted standard of right and wrong. Because propaganda maps are more likely to be global or continental rather than local, the political propagandist has a greater opportunity than either the advertiser or the real-estate developer to distort reality by manipulating the projection and framing of the map....

CARTOGRAPHIC ICONS BIG AND
SMALL: MAPS AS SYMBOLS OF
POWER AND NATIONHOOD
The map is the perfect symbol of the state. If your grand duchy or tribal area seems tired, run-down, and frayed at the edges, simply take a sheet of paper, plot some cities, roads, and physical features, draw a heavy, distinct boundary around as much territory as you dare claim, color it in, and a name—perhaps reinforced with the impressive prefix "Republic of"—and presto: you are now the leader of a new sovereign, autonomous country. Should anyone doubt it, merely point to the map. Not only is your new state on paper, it's on a map, so it must be real.

If this map-as-symbol of the state concept seems farfetched, consider the national atlases of England and France produced in the late sixteenth century. Elizabeth I of England commissioned Christopher Saxton to carry out a countrywide topographic survey of

India's version

Pakistan's version

Two official government tourist maps show Kashmir as a part of India, above, and as a part of Pakistan, below. In reality, India controls the southern part of the state of Kashmir, Pakistan controls the northwestern part, and China controls three sections along the eastern margin.

England and Wales and to publish the maps in an elaborate hand-colored atlas. In addition to providing information useful to governing her kingdom, the

atlas bound together maps of the various English counties and asserted their unity under Elizabeth's rule. Rich in symbolism, the atlas's frontispiece was a heavily decorated engraving that identified the queen as a patron of geography and astronomy. A few decades later Henry IV of France celebrated the recent reunification of his kingdom by commissioning bookseller Maurice Bouguereau to prepare a similarly detailed and decorated atlas. Like Saxton's atlas, *Le théâtre françoys* includes an impressive engraving, proclaiming the glory of king and kingdom. In both atlases regional maps provided geographic detail and a single overview map of the entire country asserted national unity.

The spate of newly independent states formed after World War II revived the national atlas as a symbol of nationhood. Although a few countries in western Europe and North America had state-sponsored national atlases in the late nineteenth and early twentieth centuries, these served largely as reference works and symbols of scientific achievement. But between 1940 and 1980 the number of national atlases increased from fewer than twenty to more than eighty, as former colonies turned to cartography as a tool of both economic development and political identity. In the service of the state, maps and atlases often play dual roles.

Perhaps the haste of new nations to assert their independence cartographically reflects the colonial powers' use of the map as an intellectual tool for legitimizing territorial conquest, economic exploitation, and cultural imperialism. Maps made it easy for European states to carve up Africa and other heathen lands, to lay claim to land and resources, and to ignore existing social and political structures. Knowledge is power, and crude explorers' maps made possible treaties between nations with conflicting claims. That maps drawn up by diplomats and generals became a political reality lends an unintended irony to the aphorism that the pen is mightier than the sword.

Nowhere is the map more a national symbol and an intellectual weapon than in disputes over territory. When nation A and nation B both claim territory C, they usually are at war cartographically as well. Nation A, which defeated nation B several decades ago and now holds territory C, has incorporated C into A on its maps. If A's maps identify C at all, they tend to mention it only when they label other provinces or subregions. If nation B was badly beaten, its maps might show C as a disputed territory. Unlike A's maps, B's maps always name C. If B feels better prepared for battle or believes internal turmoil has weakened A, B's maps might more boldly deny political reality by graphically annexing C.

Neutral countries tread a thin cartographic line by coloring or shading the disputed area to reflect A's occupation and perhaps including in smaller type a note recognizing B's claim. If A and B have different names for C, A's name appears, sometimes with B's name in parentheses. (Even when recapture by B is improbable, mapmakers like to hedge their bets.) Cartographic neutrality can be difficult, though, for customs officials of nation B sometimes embargo publications that accept as unquestioned A's sovereignty over C. If A's rule is secure, its censors can be more tolerant.

Consider, for example, the disputed state of Jammu and Kashmir, lying between India, Pakistan, and China. Both India and Pakistan claimed Kashmir, once a separate monarchy, and went to war over the area in August 1965. [A] U.S. State Department map shows the cease-fire line of fall 1965, which placed Pakistan in control of northwestern Kashmir and showed India in control of the southern portion. (China occupied a portion of northeastern Kashmir.) Nonetheless, Indian and Pakistani maps continued to deny political reality. A 1984 Pakistani government tourist map, for instance, included Kashmir in Pakistan, whereas a map in an Indian government tourist brochure ceded the entire territory to India. American and British atlases attempted to resolve the dispute with notes identifying the area occupied by Pakistan and claimed by India, the area occupied by India and claimed by Pakistan, three areas occupied by China and claimed by both India and Pakistan, the area occupied by China and claimed by India, and the area occupied by India and claimed by China. And for years publishers found it difficult to export the same books on South Asian geography to both India and Pakistan.

Mark Monmonier,
How to Lie with Maps, 2d ed., 1996

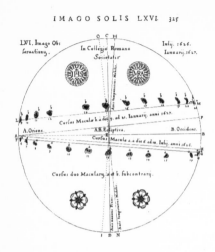

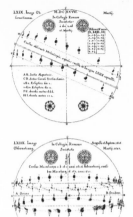

Presenting information visually

The innovative scholar Edward Tufte is a student of statistics, political science, and graphic design. In the following excerpts from two books he explores the ways various disciplines use graphics, beginning with two 17th-century astronomical illustrations and a modern physics diagram.

ESCAPING FLATLAND

Christopher Scheiner's diagram from *Rosa Ursina sive Sol*, completed in 1630, arrays the apparent path of spots across a stationary disk, an ingenious method for tracking simple sunspot structures but tending to jumble up complex data. Symbols of Scheiner's patron and religious order decorate those areas without spots in a hundred such diagrams, a reminder of Jonathan Swift's indictment of 17th-century cartographers who substituted embellishment for data:

*I*mago Solis, a sequence of diagrams from Christopher Scheiner, *Rosa Ursina sive Sol*, 1626–30.

With savage pictures fill their gaps,
And o'er unhabitable downs,
Place elephants for want of towns

These symbols, similar to a modern trademark or logotype, may have served as a seal of validation for the readers of 1630. Today they appear somewhat strident, contradicting nature's rich pattern....

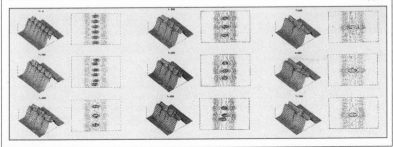

SMALL MULTIPLES

In this splendid 1659 drawing by Christiaan Huygens, the inner ellipse traces Earth's yearly journey around the Sun; the larger ellipse shows Saturn's orbit, viewed from the heavens. The outermost images depict Saturn as seen through telescopes located on Earth. All told, we have 32 Saturns, at different locations in three-space and from the perspective of two different observers—a superior *small multiple* design.

At the heart of quantitative reasoning is a single question: *Compared to what?*

A diagram by A. Ghizzo, B. Izrar, P. Bertrand, E. Fijalkow, M. R. Feix, and M. Shoucri, "Stability of Bernstein-Greene-Kruskal Plasma Equilibria: Numerical Experiments over a Long Time," from *Physics of Fluids* 31, January 1988. Viewing these illustrations upside down turns the mountains into valleys. Note also the two-space contour plots to the right of the three-space perspectives.

Christiaan Huygens, diagram from the *Systema Saturnium,* 1659.

Small multiple designs, multivariate and data bountiful, answer directly by visually enforcing comparisons of changes, of the differences among objects, of the scope of alternatives. For a wide range of problems in data presentation, small multiples are the best design solution.

Illustrations of postage-stamp size are indexed by category or a label, sequenced over time like the frames of a movie, or ordered by a quantitative variable not used in the single image itself. Information slices are positioned within the eyespan, so that viewers make comparisons at a glance—uninterrupted visual reasoning. Constancy of design puts the emphasis on changes in data, not changes in data frames.

Edward R. Tufte,
Envisioning Information,
1990

Images and quantities

Images as varied as a documentary photograph, medieval Chinese map, and a 17th-century European graph convey concrete data in different ways.

Our thinking is filled with assessments of quantity, an approximate or exact sense of number, amount, size, scale. In scientific work, both order-of-magnitude reasoning and precise measurements are pervasive. How are such quantities represented in visual expressions of ideas, experience, evidence? How are moving images, photographs, diagrams, maps, and charts to be scaled and labeled? And what makes images quantitatively eloquent?

Visual techniques for depicting quantities include *direct labels* (for example, the numerically labeled grids of statistical graphics…); *encodings* (color scales); and *self-representing scales* (objects of known size appearing in an image). Using all these methods, Josef Koudelka's haunting and vehement photograph, *The Urge to See,* testifies to the empty streets during the 1968 Soviet invasion of Czechoslovakia that ended the Prague Spring of democratic reform. In the foreground,

Josef Koudelka, *The Urge to See,* Prague, 22 August 1968. On 20 August 1968, at about 11:00 PM, troops of the Soviet Union, the Polish People's Republic, the German Democratic Republic, and the Peoples' Republic of Bulgaria crossed the border of Czechoslovakia (now the Czech Republic) and moved into Prague. On 22 August a demonstration was planned at Wenceslas Square, but it was called off. The Czechs understood that this demonstration was expected by the occupational forces as a means to repress the demonstrators and arrest their leaders. People already present were advised to abandon the square to Russian soldiers and their tanks, lining the curbs under the trees. The watch on the photographer's left arm shows 6:00 PM, and the streets are empty.

a watch documents the hour (*direct label*), as the shadows and gray light hint at the time of day (*encoding*), while in the distance Soviet tanks surround the parliament building (*self-representing scales,* as many familiar objects in perspective demarcate the street and the photographer's location).

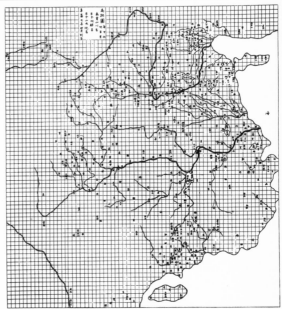

The *Yu ji tu,* or *Map of the Tracks of Yu,* Chinese, c. AD 1100. The original stone engraving is 32 x 31 inches (80 x 79 cm). The map is "the most remarkable cartographic work of its age in any culture, carved in stone in +1137 but probably dating from before +1100....The coastal outline is relatively firm and the precision of the network of river systems extraordinary....Anyone who compares this map with the contemporary productions of European religious cosmography cannot but be amazed at the extent to which Chinese geography was at that time ahead of the West....There was nothing like it in Europe till the Escorial MS. map of about +1550."

Joseph Needham,
Science and Civilization in China,
vol. 3: *Mathematics and the Sciences of
the Heavens and the Earth,* 1959

Maps express quantities visually by location (two-dimensional addresses of latitude and longitude) and by areal extent (surface coverage). Some 900 years ago a fully scaled map was engraved in stone by precocious Chinese cartographers....A note on the stone indicates that each grid square represents 100 *li,* a scale of map to world of approximately 1 to 4,500,000.

Despite their quantifying scales and grids, maps resemble miniature pictorial representations of the physical world. To depict relations between *any* measured quantities, however, requires replacing the map's natural spatial scales with abstract scales of measurement not based on geographic analogy.

To go from maps of existing scenery to graphs of newly measured and collated data was an enormous conceptual step. Embodied in the very first maps were all the ideas necessary for making statistical graphics—quantified measures of locations of nouns in two-dimensional space—and yet it took

5,000 years to change the name of the coordinates from *west-east* and *north-south* to empirically measured variables *X* and *Y*. The even longer history of art took a similar course: the naturalistic coordinate system of painted cave-wall and canvas was first dislocated by Cubism's fractured images from multiple viewpoints and then eventually abandoned altogether in 20th-century abstract painting, as the two dimensions of the canvas no longer referred to worldly scenery but

the chart cites the astronomers and cartographers making the estimates— Jansson, Mercator, Schoener, Lansberge, Brahe, Regiomontanus, Ptolemy, and others. On Langren's scale, the broadly inexact position of Rome, sprawled out 22° to 25° from Toledo, places it far east of its actual location and well across the Adriatic Sea into western Greece. A one-dimensional map of data, the chart is remarkably advanced for its time, spatially arranging (rather than merely

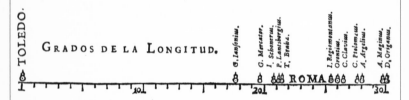

M ichael Florent van Langren, diagram from *La Verdadera longitud por mar y tierra,* 1644. The purpose of the graph was to advance Langren's own method for the determination of longitude because of "the existence of such enormous errors, as can be seen from the line, which shows the different distances that the greatest astronomers and geographers put between Rome and Toledo."

only to themselves.

One of the earliest visual representations of statistical data was drawn in 1644 by Michael Florent van Langren, a Flemish astronomer to the Spanish court. Appropriately enough for statistics, this graph shows 12 diverse estimates of the distance between Toledo and Rome. Measured in degrees longitude, the scale locates Toledo, the historic Spanish city portrayed in El Greco's *View of Toledo,* at the prime meridian of 0°. All the longitudes are too large, perhaps a result of underestimating the earth's circumference. The correct distance is 16° 30'. Combining nouns with numbers,

recording in a table) various estimates of the same quantity. Furthermore, the data are distributed in relation to a putatively true value. Langren's chart appears to be the earliest display of a distribution of common measurements; and it is my candidate for the first statistical graphic ever.

Edward R. Tufte,
Visual Explanations:
Images and Quantities,
Evidence and Narrative,
1997

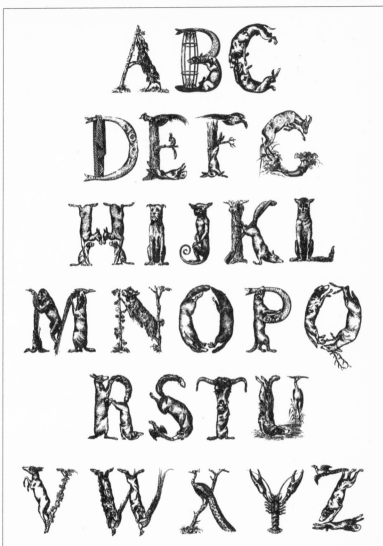

A fanciful design for letters of the alphabet conveys both visual and verbal information.

Further Reading

SIGN THEORY

Baron, N., *Speech, Writing and Sign: A Functional View of Linguistic Representation*, 1980

Barthes, R., *Empire of Signs*, trans. R. Howard, 1982

————, *The Pleasure of the Text*, trans. R. Miller, 1975

Eco, U. *A Theory of Semiotics*, 1976

————, *Semiotics and the Philosophy of Language*, 1984

Eliade, M., *Patterns in Comparative Religion*, trans. R. Sheed, 1958

————, *A History of Religious Ideas*, trans. W. Trask, A. Hiltebeitel, and D. Apostolos-Cappadona, 3 vols., 1978, 1982, 1985

Gelb, I. J., *A Study of Writing*, rev. ed., 1963

Lévi-Strauss, C., *The Savage Mind*, 1968

————, *Structural Anthropology I*, trans. C. Jacobson and B. Grundfest Schoepf, 1963

Saussure, F. de, *Course in General Linguistics*, trans. W. Baskin, 1959

Stewart, J., ed., *Beyond the Symbol Model: Reflections of the Representational Nature of Language*, 1996

Turner, V., *The Forest of Symbols: Aspects of Ndembu Ritual*, 1967

WRITING

Campbell, G. L., *Handbook of Scripts and Alphabets*, 1997

Coulmas, F., *The Writing Systems of the World*, 1989

Gordon, C. H., *Forgotten Scripts: Their Ongoing Discovery and Decipherment*, rev. ed., 1982

Jean, G., *Writing: The Story of Alphabets and Scripts*, trans. J. Oates, 1992

Senner, W. M., ed., *The Origins of Writing*, 1989

SYMBOLS AND GRAPHICS

Bertin, J., *Graphics and Graphic Information Processing*, trans. W. J. Berg and P. Scott, 1981

Cirlot, J. E., *A Dictionary of Symbols*, trans. J. Sage, 1962

Eliade, M., *Images and Symbols: Studies in Religious Symbolism*, trans. P. Mairet, 1952

Hall, J., *Dictionary of Subjects and Symbols in Art*, rev. ed., 1979

Lehner, E., *Symbols, Signs, and Signets*, 1950

Modley, R., with Myers, W. R., *Handbook of Pictorial Symbols*, 1976

Shepherd, W., *Shepherd's Glossary of Graphic Signs and Symbols*, 1971

Todorov, T., *Theories of the Symbol*, trans. C. Porter, 1984

Tufte, E. R., *Envisioning Information*, 1990

————, *The Visual Display of Quantitative Information*, 1983

————, *Visual Explanations: Images and Quantities, Evidence and Narrative*, 1997

PREHISTORY

Abélanet, J., *Signes sans paroles*, 1986

Clottes, J., and Courtin, J., *The Cave Beneath the Sea: Paleolithic Images at Cosquer*, trans. M. Garner, 1996

Gowlett, J. A. J., *Ascent to Civilization: The Archeology of Early Humans*, 2d ed., 1993

Leroi-Gourhan, A., *Treasures of Prehistoric Art*, 1967

Vialou, D., *Prehistoric Art and Civilization*, trans. P. Bahn, 1998

White, R., *Dark Caves, Bright Visions: Life in Ice Age Europe*, exh. cat., American Museum of Natural History, New York, 1986

MAPS

Allen, P., *The Atlas of Atlases: The Map Maker's Vision of the World*, 1992

Cartes et figures de la terre, exh. cat., Centre Georges Pompidou, Paris, 1980

Fisher, H. T., *Mapping Information: The Graphic Display of Quantitative Information*, 1982

Harley, J. B., and Woodward, D. eds., *The History of Cartography*, 6 vols., 1987–

Keates, J. S., *Understanding Maps*, 1982

MacEachren, A., M., *How Maps Work: Representation, Visualization, and Design*, 1995

Monmonier, M., *How to Lie with Maps*, 2d ed., 1996

Muehrcke, P. C., and J. O., *Map Use: Reading, Analysis, and Interpretation*, 3d ed., 1992

Woodward, D., *Art and Cartography: Six Historical Essays*, 1987

CODES, BODY LANGUAGE, AND NONVERBAL LANGUAGES

Armstrong, D., Stokoe, W. C., Wilcox, S., *Gesture and the Nature of Language*, 1995

Carron, *Morse Code: The Essential Language*, 1991

Chomsky, N., *Language and Mind*, 1968

Emmorey, K., and Reilly, J., *Language, Gesture, and Space*, 1995

Klima, E. S., and Bellugi, U., *The Signs of Language*, 1979

Kyle, J. G., and Woll, B., *Sign Language: The Study of Deaf People and Their Language*, 1985

Lane, H., Hoffmeister, R., and Bahan, B., *A Journey into the Deaf World*, 1996

Lecoq, J., *Le Théâtre du geste*, 1987

Morris, D., *Manwatching: A Field Guide to Human Behavior*, 1977

Sacks, O., *Seeing Voices: A Journey into the World of the Deaf*, 1990

Schein, J. D., *Speaking the Language of Sign: The Art and Science of Signing*, 1984

Tomkins, W., *Indian Sign Language*, 1969

List of Illustrations

Key: a=above; **b**=below; **c**=center; **l**=left; **r**=right

Front cover Clockwise from *al:* decorative bar of music; terrestrial globe; detail of an engraving, Cadbury Collection of Atlases, Birmingham Central Library, England; detail from the title page of *The Astrologer of the Nineteenth Century; or, The Master Key of Futurity*, London, 1825, a book on the occult; modern reproduction of an ankh, or Egyptian amulet; detail of p. 87a; hand, engraved frontispiece to Johann Rothman, *The Art of Divining (Keiponanti'a)*, London, 1652, showing the lines of life, mind, fate, and love, and the astrological symbols relating to the mounts and plains of the hand; pyramid with eye, detail of the reverse of the United States one-dollar bill; background, *Deities from the Book of the Gates*, detail of a stone relief in the Tomb of Horemhab, c. 1320 BC, Valley of the Kings, Egypt

Spine Detail of p. 40

Back cover Left to right:

detail of p. 119a; modern danger sign, from p. 105b; detail of p. 102

Inside front cover Paul Klee, *Le Sapin (The Pine Tree)*, drawing, 1940, collection of Félix Klee, Bern

1 William Law, *The Tree of the Soul*, from *The Works of Jakob Böhme*, London, 1746–81

2a Drawing of a shaman's tent, Manchuria

2b Wood engraving, *Three Evergreens are Born from the Body of Adam after His Death, a Cypress, a Pine, and a Cedar*, from John Ashton, ed., *The Legendary History of the True Cross*, 1937

3a Drawing from a stone vase, Mesopotamia, 5th–4th century BC

3b Wood engraving, *Adam's Tree*, from John Ashton, ed., *The Legendary History of the True Cross*, 1937

4l Alexander the Great and the Tree, Persian miniature, 15th century

4r–5l The Tree of the Virtues and Vices, Lambert de Saint-Omer, miniature in the *Liber Floridus Lamberti*, Flemish, c. 1120, Ghent, Rijksuniversiteit, cod. 1125, fols. 231v—232r

5ar Stone panel engraved with dove, tree, and two anchor-crosses, early Christian symbols, Catacomb of Priscilla, Rome, 2d century AD

5r Manuscript illumination detail of a miniature from the *Beatus Commentary on the Apocalypse*, AD 975

6al Detail of an anonymous illustration, *Song of the Tree of Love*, 19th century, Bibliothèque des Arts Décoratifs, Paris

6bl Souls Transformed into Birds, manuscript illumination from a 15th-century edition of Dante, *The Divine Comedy*, Bibliothèque Marcienne, Paris

6br–7bl The Tree of Jesse, gilt-stucco decoration, Church of Santo Domingo, Oaxaca, Mexico, 17th century

7r Detail of a manuscript illumination from the *Bible of San Bidoro*, León, Spain, 10th century

9 Detail from an illustration to a 1785 edition of the hermetic text *Tabula Smaragdina* printed in Altona (Hamburg), reprinted 1919, Bibliothèque Nationale, Paris

10 Mesolithic handprints from a cave in Santa Cruz Province, Argentina, c. 9000–7000 BC

11 History of the Migration of the Aztecs, detail of a manuscript illumination in the Codex Boturini, 16th century, Museo Nacional de Antropologia, Mexico City

12 Horse with dots and negative handprints, Paleolithic cave painting, Pech-Merle cave, Lot, France, 15,000–12,000 BC

12b–13b Bison with rows of dots and hatchings, Paleolithic cave painting, Altamira cave, Santander, Spain, c. 21,000–13,000 BC

14a Antler baton with geometric designs, Paleolithic, Musée Archéologique, Gênes, France

14b Traced reconstruction of an incised-stone drawing of a man, possibly pierced by spears, Mas d'Azil cave, Ariège, France, c. 15,000–10,000 BC, from André Leroi-Gourhan, *Treasures of Prehistoric Art*, 1967

15 Four painted stones, top to bottom: two with red compartments and

S ymbols representing the twelve signs of the Zodiac, from an anonymous Hungarian *Gypsy Planet and Dream Book.*

Index

Photograph Credits

Text Credits

Georges Jean was born in Besançon, France, in 1920.
He was professor of linguistics and semiology at the
University of Maine (France) from 1967 to 1981.
He has published fifty works, including eight collections
of poems, essays on poetic and teaching theory,
and several poetry anthologies of poetry.

For N.

Translated from the French by Sophie Hawkes

For Harry N. Abrams, Inc.
Editor: Eve Sinaiko
Typographic designers: Elissa Ichiyasu, Tina Thompson, Dana Sloan
Cover designer: Dana Sloan
Text permissions: Barbara Lyons

For assistance and technical information, thanks are due to the Association
and Musée Valentin Haüy, *La Vie du Rail,* and Linda White,
Bill Moody, and Carole Lazorisak.

Library of Congress Cataloging-in-Publication Data

Jean, Georges.
　　[Langage de signes. English]
　　Signs, symbols, and ciphers / Georges Jean.
　　　　p.　　cm. — (Discoveries)
　　Includes bibliographical references and index.
　　ISBN 0–8109–2842–6 (pbk.)
　　1. Signs and symbols.　I. Title.　II. Series : Discoveries (New York, N.Y.)
P99.J3813 1998　　　　　　　　　　　　　　　　　　　　98–25087
302.2—dc21

© Gallimard 1989

English translation © 1998 Harry N. Abrams, Inc., New York

Published in 1998 by Harry N. Abrams, Incorporated, New York

Printed and bound in Italy by Editoriale Libraria, Trieste